Fresh Water from Old Wells

A NEW LOOK AT BIBLICAL STORIES
THAT MAY HAVE CONFUSED YOU

Rev. John Hay Nichols

Rev. John Hay Nichols
12 Coltsway
Wayland, MA 01778

Unless noted otherwise, all Biblical quotations are from *The HarperCollins Study Bible: New Revised Standard Version, with the Apocryphal/Deuterocanonical Books* (eds. Wayne A. Meeks et al.; New York: HarperCollins, 1993).

Book Layout ©2017 BookDesignTemplates.com
Photo of John Nichols ©2007 DamianosPhotography.com

Fresh Water from Old Wells/ Rev. John Hay Nichols. —1st ed.
ISBN 978-1-6953601-1-2

Contents

This book is dedicated to my editor Bev Koteff, who has saved me many an awkward sentence and to her husband Bill, who has provided tech support through two books. As well, it could not have been written but for my wife Nancy, who has seen me through two books with patience and love.

Preface

As a parish minister, I have spent my professional life trying to help people connect with the deepest sources of their spiritual lives. I have found that one of the best ways of doing this is by telling stories. We tend to relax more when we listen to stories, and we are more receptive to what someone else is saying. Stories tend to invite the listener into shared thought with the speaker. We wonder if there is any other way this story could have turned out. Is there anything I would have done to make this situation different? Have I ever been in a situation like this? Preaching – in contrast to storytelling – tends to pose only two alternatives: accept it or reject it.

Many of the stories in the Bible are wonderful for storytelling, even though too often they are heard in the accept/reject mood. When I realized that stories opened up a world of thoughts, questions, and even some answers, I used them in my sermons more and more. Many people liked them and suggested I should have them published. At the time, I was sure no commercial publisher would have considered publishing a volume of sermons, and self-publishing seemed like a very expensive proposition. That is no longer the case.

So I lay before you some of my favorite sermons, most of which use stories from the Bible as a basis for reflection. These stories are from the Jewish and Christian scriptures and appear in the order in which they are situated in the Bible. I have also written three chapters that are not sermons, but they are included because they also make important contributions to the Western literary tradition.

Since most of these chapters were first written to be heard, they are written to entertain as well as put some serious questions and ideas forward. The mood is a little lighter than you might expect. My aim is to help readers relax and enjoy the story without entering into the seriousness of being "preached at" that drove many people from their home church into the congregations I have served. And the lighter mood is my style anyway.

Some of these sermons were first preached several years ago. They have been reworked several times since. At this point, I am not sure where some of the ideas I worked with originated, and I have not tried to track them down. A difference between preaching and academic work is that preachers have the responsibility to make their thoughts live rather than creep along in constant homage to the academic sources from which they came.

Thus it was with Martin Luther King Jr.'s comment that "the arc of the universe is long but it bends toward justice." King is actually quoting the words of nineteenth-century Unitarian minister Theodore Parker. But King made that quotation sing by not footnoting the author. In a similar vein, don't assume that all the ideas I present are mine alone.

If any part of this book intrigues you, it will have achieved my purpose. If you find that you enjoyed several of these sermons, the book will have achieved its goal. The experience and passion of generations reaches out to you.

—REV. JOHN HAY NICHOLS

CHAPTER 1

The Story of an Old Well

This book contains my reflections on some of the stories that come from the Bible. But this chapter is an explanation in story form of how I believe the scriptures came to be written and appreciated, used, and perhaps misused. Reading this story literally will yield little of any value. Let your imagination play with mine, and you can catch my meaning.

O nce in the midst of a long trail across an arid desert, there was a well of life-giving water. Travelers looked forward to stopping there, because tasting the water from this well filled them with confidence about the sweetness of life. They went away refreshed but also renewed in strength, enthusiasm, and insight. For this reason, they came to believe that the stream that fed the well flowed from God.

Some travelers decided there was no better place on earth to live than beside this well. They brought their families, their tents and flocks, and they settled there. A small community was formed. To order their lives together and as a way of learning to trust one another, they developed rituals for sharing the well water. The rituals also helped their children understand how the parents had found the water and what it had meant to them.

Eventually, a large village grew up around the oasis, and many became concerned that the popularity of the water source would destroy its freshness. So they constructed walls around the well and restricted access to it. Travelers were still allowed to come and taste the water, but first they had to learn the rituals of water tasting. The rituals seemed to multiply in number with each generation. Eventually, observing the rites and rituals of the well keepers became more important to them than sharing the water itself.

Still, the travelers came to sample the water from the well. The villagers formed an institution to deal with the well's new popularity. However, as the institution became more powerful, differences arose. Various factions within the well-keeping institution began to quarrel over who had the right to guard the water source and offer drinks from it. Eventually, each faction went away and dug its own well, attempting to draw off water from the original source.

Each group now claimed it had the real water. As a way of consolidating their power, they set up rules and restrictions governing who had the right to draw up the water, who had the right to sip from it, who had the right to control the whole situation, and who had the right to consult with the boss. Eventually, the groups began to form their separate identities. They were called orthodox, conservative, reformed, moderate, and liberal. Later they were called Jews, Christians, and followers of Islam. Still later, they would be called Catholics, Episcopalians, Methodists, Lutherans, Baptists, Puritans, and Separatists. The Jews among them would be called Orthodox, Conservative, and Reformed along with other distinctions.

As the factions guarding the water became even larger, more powerful, and more opposed to each other, they paved over many times the area where the oasis had been. In its place they built large houses in which to worship the value of well keeping. In time, they even forgot where the water was located. But they remembered the stories and fragments of stories that had been told and passed down to them by the people who had once actually seen the fresh water and had tasted it.

The language in which these stories were first told was lost. Some details in the stories had been modified in the many retellings. Somewhere in the transitions between generations, many people lost the ability to listen to stories in ways that would make their meanings live for a new age. Nonetheless, the stories survived. For a few, they carried a hint of the freshness that convinced the first travelers to return over and over to the oasis. The very fact that they survived suggests that they sounded true chords with the people who preserved them and passed them along.

Nevertheless, it is fair to say that many were and are indifferent to the well tradition, and some now are openly hostile, particularly among those who understand themselves as either religiously liberal or secular. The stories of the well continue to be told but are heard with far less impact than they once had.

They are inscribed now in small print on tissue-thin pages in books that are handed out as graduation presents and rarely opened again. Their richness has been lost on many who, not having learned how to listen to the stories and incorporate them into their lives, have begun to wonder if there ever really was a source of fresh water. Or was it all a pre-scientific illusion?

Those favoring the illusion point of view have said, "There never was a well. The whole thing is a myth, and the purpose of the myth was to sustain the well keepers in power so that they could oppress other people. We are better off without the entire tradition. So let us go bravely forth and learn to live without any hope of sustenance from the oasis."

Folks on the other extreme, calling themselves conservatives or fundamentalists, have said, "Of course there is a well. There is a source of living water, and it is without question everything we say it is, but you can approach it only in one way, which is our way. It can mean only what we say it means."

And a few have suggested, "Let us go and dig a new well for ourselves. When we find the water, we will then create a new religious language, new rituals, and new communities that do not oppress people, as we now believe the old well keepers did. Let us then do away with the old language and traditions as they only impede or delay the birth of the new."

As a Unitarian Universalist minister, I often speak to those who question whether the Biblical tradition holds anything worth plumbing for, and I speak to many who have chosen to look elsewhere than in the Bible for inspiration and strength. Some of my colleagues would be reckoned among those who hope for the creation of a new tradition that will not carry the centuries of "baggage" of contemporary Christianity. They are also offended by the claims of some Christian and Jewish theologians that their truth is exclusive – that no one gets a drink from the well except those aligning with them.

I believe that the essence of the three traditional Western religions – Judaism, Islam, and Christianity – comes from the same well, which could refresh and strengthen us, open our eyes, and teach us. But each tradition is layered over by centuries of interpretations and translations of translations of passages and stories. To find the source or meaning of these passages and stories, we must encounter them as if they had several layers of meaning. The traditions from this well were never intended for passive consumption. They were written to be discussed, imagined, and tried out against the demands of our own spiritual lives.

This requires that we be willing to enter into the discipline of becoming familiar with one tradition. I have chosen the Judaic and Christian traditions, and I have tried to learn them thoroughly enough to be able to draw the deeper meanings from the well. However, many religious seekers today tend to flit from one tradition to another. In so doing, they find only what is on the surface. What is on the surface of any well-keeping tradition is not enough to sustain us, though it can be enough to create misunderstanding and frustration.

Here is an example. In Matthew 5:48 (KJV), Jesus says, "Be ye perfect therefore as your heavenly father is perfect." For people who consider themselves outside of any well-keeping tradition, this may have been one of the problematic passages that turned them away from the Christian scriptures. Perfection seems an impossible goal, and the memoirs of many men and women who grew up with this yardstick held over them reflect how bitterly they struggled with it.

No passage did more to estrange me from the teachings and the person of Jesus. Perfect! I was having a hard-enough time becoming just nice or caring, but perfection didn't seem to be in the cards. I wondered how I could reverence someone who thought perfection was even remotely possible for me or for anyone I knew.

As it turned out, "perfection" is probably the wrong word for understanding the passage. It may be a mistranslation. In the sentences that precede these words, Jesus tells his disciples that if they are nice only to those who are nice to them, that is just a business arrangement. Then he asks them that if they forgive only those who are forgiving, what have they accomplished? For a real spiritual discipline, he suggests, try being generous – not "perfect," the word is "generous" – even to those who do not return your generosity.

Other translations use the words "merciful," "compassionate," and "mature." In fact, if we peel away the centuries of assumptions we've made based on a particular translator's choice of words, we get closer to the source of the fresh water. The text is saying to us that the only way to find lasting peace is to reflect God's generosity to us and to all Creation through our own generosity to others. Generosity, or the lack of it, is something we do understand in ourselves and in others. But how much pain has been caused by the misuse of the word "perfection" where the words "kindness" and "generosity" would have brought us closer to the well of living water?

Nonetheless, we are not going to wade into the vagaries of different translations in the text of this book. Instead, I will try to engage you to imagine how different passages of the Bible reflect and perhaps illuminate our own times and dilemmas. In the next chapter, we will start with what are probably the most misunderstood and maligned stories from the Bible.

CHAPTER 2

Illusions of Perfection

I've found it very difficult to encourage people to look at the story of Adam and Eve differently from what they expect to hear, the way the story is written. Because Eve ate of the forbidden fruit and tempted Adam to do so, she and Adam fell from the grace of God. An angry God punished them both and sentenced them and all other men and women to lives of pain and toil. There is another way of reading the story.

I did not attend my thirtieth college reunion nor did any of my friends. But when the letters came summoning each of us to a weekend of incredible fun at our alma mater, we all decided we at least ought to call each other. When we graduated, we were sure we would remain in close touch. But our careers, families, a fair amount of physical distance, and the normal dumb urgencies of daily life intervened.

The substance of our phone calls revealed that on the surface we had done pretty well. We had fulfilled many of the goals we had when we graduated: marriage, advancement, and recognition. And there were other less pleasant lessons we learned through the usual painful experiences of growing up.

We also found that we still liked each other, and we promised to actually get together.

But there was one old friend among the missing. Each of us thought the others must be in touch with him, but no one had heard from him. Not even the alumni office had an address. This seemed odd, because he was the one among us who had most valued friendship and loyalty. I had a nagging thought that he was absent because he was hiding and did not want to be found.

Sometime later, while I was visiting with my former sophomore roommate, we found an internet search engine that scanned public telephone directories; we gave it a try. We discovered six phone numbers for this name, one of which looked very promising. I wrote it down intending to try it, though I still had the nagging feeling that quite possibly our friend did not want to be found. As it turned out, I was right.

He had been hiding, but something about deciding whether or not to return my phone call made him decide that perhaps it was time to be found. He told me that shortly after leaving graduate school, a love affair went sour and depressed him seriously. Much later, he discovered that depression was a tendency that ran in his family. Not knowing this for quite a while, he took his depression to be further proof of his worthlessness as a person.

Publicly, he managed to do fairly well, though privately he "shut down," in his words, from any relationships that could turn out to be disappointing. Instead, he turned to an addiction that eventually took over his life, caused him to fall from grace professionally, and then to become embarrassed in the community where he lived. He now has serious health problems, and his prospects for continuing in his profession are not good.

After graduation, we parted with tickets to graduate school in our hands and bright prospects ahead. The fighting in

Vietnam had not yet become a daily feature on the six o'clock news, and we had no idea that it would reach our lives. The future stretched before us – clear, promising, and fairly simple. Work hard, follow the rules, and you will end up on top. Of course, we all believed we had the wit, wisdom, and attractiveness to do just that. But many years later, things do not seem that simple for anyone.

Nearly everyone I know who has been willing to confide in me has told of sleepless nights beyond counting spent over serious threats to them professionally, deep feelings of self-doubt over the damage they've done to cherished relationships with partners and children, over grief that is old, anticipated, or new. One of the reasons we cannot build enough bridges of understanding and forgiveness is that we have often failed to keep the bridges we did build in good repair.

In the Jewish tradition, there is a period of time called the High Holy Days that is a time for repairing those bridges. It is a time – like Christmas or Easter for many gentiles – that promises a new start. The High Holy Days often draw congregants who do not normally frequent the synagogue back to corporate worship as well as to family celebrations. These rituals recognize that however far people have fallen from their own best intentions, there is a chance to repair what has been ripped or frayed and perhaps even to mend what has been broken. Rosh Hashanah brings worshippers back to the dawn of creation, to the beginning of a new year and a newly rededicated life.

A rededicated life! What would that mean? At the very least, it means trying to achieve some sort of reconciliation with the people we have hurt or wronged. A rededicated life means looking more closely at what we believe, what we do, and what we do that makes us and the people around us happy or unhappy.

Many people, like my good friend and former classmate, believe that there is only one road that leads to the good life for all people. Many believe this road is well paved, well traveled, and very clearly marked. If we find ourselves wandering around in the boonies of life rather than on the throughway, it must be because we have stupidly lost our way and so we deserve to be lost. Good people, thoughtful people, ambitious people, hard-working people, and people of whom we approve do not ever, ever get lost on the way to their goals – so we try to convince ourselves.

These illusions of perfection – which we often protest that we do not hold – are nonetheless squirreled away in our psyches, because we live in a culture that is strongly influenced by a conservative interpretation of the story of Adam and Eve. We have been told that the moral of this story is that the first man and woman messed up. They messed up because they disobeyed a perfectly sensible rule that they should not eat of the Tree of the Knowledge of Good and Evil. Thus, they gravely disappointed God who then threw a temper tantrum and cast them out of the Garden of Eden, condemning them to lives of misery, which they richly deserved.

It almost no longer matters whether people believe in this sort of God or in this understanding of the story, because we already have it in our heads that if we mess up, if we violate a perfectly sensible rule, then we get punished somehow. We get pain, and we deserve all of it because we have offended God and humanity who are not very forgiving.

There is another way of looking at the story and at our lives. It appears in Rabbi Kushner's book *How Good Do We Have to Be?* It could well be that the traditional interpretation that has left its heavy footprint on many people is wrong. Perhaps, God placed these two carefree creatures in the Garden of Eden. But as God watched them cavort in the Garden with no more self-consciousness than two playful terriers, with no more purpose in life than to eat until they were full, with no greater moral commitment to one another than two toddlers in a sandbox, God realized this was not quite the vision of humanity that was intended.

So perhaps God gave Adam and Eve a choice. God said, "You can become carefree but uncomplicated creatures like so many other creatures I've made, or you can become human beings." And God was actually relieved when Adam and Eve chose as they did to obtain the knowledge of good and evil. God then said:

> Now that you have chosen to be human, this is what it means: you will work hard to earn a living. This will bring anxiety and frustration but also reward.

> You will make mistakes, even mistakes big enough to be terrifying, but you can learn from them. And if you learn that life is full of mistakes, you will learn compassion for other people. Now you will also know the pain of birth, but your children will become more important to you than children are to many of my creatures. Now you will have to mourn, but in doing so you will begin to take what you have been given more seriously. Now you will know that you cannot live forever. But knowing that, you will find each day more precious.

Imagine the difference in our thinking if this story had been understood differently from believing that original sin was disobedience, that the consequences were horrendous, and that the only way to get back into God's good graces was to follow what men and women were told were "the rules." Many people grew up with the idea that there were certain fixed standards of success against which all must be measured up or be damned. Failing to measure up completely – and all of us will fail in some way – everyone fell into the habit of blaming other people and themselves. Many – and my good friend almost got included in that number – finally decided they were so far out of Eden that there was no acceptance of any kind that would be possible for them.

Imagine instead a world in which we all learned some compassion for ourselves and for others, a world in which a mistake, however tragic, did not become a crushing defeat. Imagine a world in which we truly understand that there is not one straight-and-narrow road to happiness, but there are many. Those who may be off exploring various sideroads may be on a route that will be just as fulfilling for them as the one we have chosen for ourselves. Imagine a world in which joy, love, compassion, and moral commitment grow genuinely out of a life experience that has taught us how much we need each other.

Imagine a world in which we give up our illusions of perfection. We would understand that the people with whom we share our lives struggle, as we do, to be their best selves. Sometimes they are embarrassed when they do not succeed. Imagine that in this world our children will never be to us the embodiment of what has been left unfulfilled in our lives. They will always be on their own journeys. It would be hurtful for us to try and raise them otherwise.

We would understand as well that our parents were probably better parents at some stages of their lives than at others, and that they never could be the parents we wish we had, just as we could not have been the children they thought they should have had. Finally, imagine a world in which we could understand and appreciate one another for the talents we do have rather than for the talents we do not have.

This is not yet the world we live in, which is why it is so difficult to imagine these things ever coming to pass. Sometimes, we pay a terrible price in failed dreams and in broken lives.

In defense of the scriptures, they never said Adam and Eve's difficulties were a fall from anything. They identify the first sin several chapters later in talking about Cain and Abel. Cain is convinced that Abel's offering has been more acceptable to God than his own. He expresses his resentment, and God warns him that sin is crouching at the door. The sin God means is resentment and rivalry. But God implies that you can master it when you discover that there is enough love in the world for both of you.

As we move through the stories of Genesis, we discover the rivalry of Isaac and Ishmael, Jacob and Esau, Joseph and his brothers. In fact, the entire book of Genesis is about the rivalries of siblings failing to understand that there is enough happiness, power, and love for everyone. Yet, at the end of each story, a reconciliation occurs. Isaac and Ishmael, bitterly separated for years because Ishmael and his mother had been cast out of the family in favor of Isaac, are reunited when Abraham dies, and they bury their father together.

Jacob, who cheated his brother Esau and just about everyone else, returns to Esau after many years of having been tossed around in the world. Because the two men have now formed lives that are independent of their father's disputed blessing, they are able to be reconciled. Joseph, given the opportunity to do unto his brothers as they had so cruelly done to him, chose to forgive them as they most likely forgave him for having been such a self-absorbed jerk of a younger brother.

There is a message here. The great sin is not disobedience. The great sin is becoming so caught in our illusions of perfection and self-righteousness that we do not realize the love that is offered to us, the opportunities we have to companion others through the shadowy valleys that await everyone, and the humanity that unites all of us.

My missing friend told me that at the lowest point of his difficulties – a time when he was held up to suspicion and scorn in the community — members of the small congregation where he worshipped gathered around him. They said, "Pay no attention to what other people say. We know who you are, and we know that you are loved." That is how he learned that his perfectionist aspirations had been his illusion, and that their love was real.

CHAPTER 3

Pride and Her Children

Genesis 11 tells what at first seems like a silly little story in which God throws a temper tantrum and destroys the tower that the people of the world have built to reach to the heavens. God then confuses their languages so that they cannot easily communicate and build another tower. Can God be so insecure as to rain on his children's parade? Or does the story make a more important point?

The story in Genesis 11 begins in a time when everyone spoke one language and lived in one place. Being ambitious, they learned to make bricks and build with them. They got so good at it that they built a tower with its top in the heavens. One day, God came down, saw the tower, and realized that if this sort of thing were to continue, the people of the earth would have power far exceeding their ability to use it wisely. So, God halted the Tower of Babel project then and there, and he scattered the pieces to the winds. God also confused their language so that they would never again be able to work together enough to mount another assault on heaven.

Many people might read this story and think, "Well there he goes again: God the petty tyrant. Once his kids get a few original ideas, he clamps down on them like a Nazi commandant. He scatters his creations far and wide and sends the children to their rooms." In this story, God is like the father who grounds his teenage son for a year because the boy came back only five minutes late for a curfew. Was it so important, in this instance, that God show who's boss?

That's one way to look at the story. But it is a more complicated story than that. I am dedicated to convincing you that the ancients were just as smart as we are and have a great deal to say to us — despite not having had the advantages of a contemporary education. Let me give you some of the background for the story.

In the period before the Hebrews compiled some of their earliest scriptures, their land was conquered. Their leaders were captured and taken to Babylon where they remained for many years; that experience influenced many parts of the story we read in Genesis. This Babylonian captivity of the Hebrew leadership was a painful mix of two cultures: the Hebrew culture characterized by a rigid idealism and the Babylonian culture characterized by cynicism.

Their Babylonian captors had enjoyed absolute power for a long time. In nearly every way, they were at the top of the Middle Eastern pile. They began to believe they were the political, intellectual, and spiritual pinnacles of human achievement. There was nothing greater than they were — so they believed.

They recognized no power greater than theirs. But that power was only as real as the statues that had been made for them. Their gods were really figures of speech: poetic conceits, objects of art, or at best, icons for the common person. But these gods were certainly not any serious influence over the lives of the Babylonian leaders with whom the Jews came in contact.

The Jews, who became authors of the book of Genesis, believed that their Babylonian captors were not happy in their own lives. They had a kind of "been there, done that" attitude toward just about everything. They were wrapped with the cynicism that comes upon people who have elevated their own ambitions, goals, and security into their only major concern. Therefore, the Babylonian intellectuals had discovered – but could not admit to themselves – what a puny thing, what a small, anxious, quivering thing the individual ego is. This knowledge bored and saddened them.

These Babylonians had actually built a large tower – maybe four or five stories tall by today's terms – certainly a huge tower for that time, reaching as close to the heavens as anyone could imagine being. They called it "bab-il," meaning a gate to God. But the Hebrews thought the Babylonian presumption that they could actually storm the gates of heaven was a large portion of what deprived their captors of hopefulness or joy. They thought they had to control everything. They had no appreciation of a life that was surrounded by gifts coming from a mysterious creativity that was forever out of bounds, unreachable, and uncontrollable.

We might say the Babylonians were burdened by their own lives and even in despair, but the Hebrews called it confusion. When they returned to Israel from their years of captivity, they retold the story of the tower they saw that stormed the gates of heaven but described it using the Hebrew word "babel," which means "confusion." The story of their encounter with this tower became one of the ways in which they remembered how they developed their religious beliefs about the dangers of pride and the worship of idols.

The harsh realism of the Biblical voice sometimes needs to cross a bridge of translation in order to reach us, because we often think our world is too far removed from the past for there to be a crossover from that world to our understanding. In addition, the Bible speaks very harshly – as in this story – about the dangers of pride. Yet in the last thirty years, psychologists and educators have been trying hard to encourage people to take more pride in themselves.

The movement to teach by affirming pride and self-esteem caught momentum when I was entering the ministry. It has flowered for over forty years. I can appreciate why it began and why it is important. It went way too far. It is important for us to feel good about ourselves, but your self and my self are just too fragile to be the only containers we have for our lives' deeper meanings or the only source we have for hopefulness.

The Biblical critique of a world in which self-esteem and self-enhancement are the highest goals is that if your view of the world has you at the center of it, then it is not only false, it is also too small a world for you to live in. It doesn't work. It is both confining and misleading. Our lives are always contingent upon the efforts of others as well as the efforts we make and the commitments we keep. We depend upon the whole larger scheme of Living Creation, whose children we are and with which we will eventually be reunited.

This great mystery challenges us, surprises and strengthens us, and – if we will allow it – can bring us peace when we accept that we alone are not responsible for bringing good things into our lives. We are part of a much larger scheme of Creation or Divinity in which we have a role to play and a place of honor, and in which we are loved.

The Hebrews were also concerned about the pride that is a pretense we make: a pretense that we are never uncertain or confused; a pretense that we are never caught by our own limitations; a pretense that we will never reach that point at which we feel helpless to resolve something. Such pride places all of our hopes in the too-fragile vessel of our unaided ability, wisdom, and judgment.

The extent to which our hyperventilated self-esteem sometimes blinds us can be amusing. Several years ago, the College Entrance Examination Board invited one million high school seniors to answer the question, "How do you feel you compare with other people your own age in areas of ability?" They felt quite good, as it turned out. Sixty percent reported themselves "better than average'" in athletic ability. Only six percent reported themselves "below average." Seventy percent rated themselves "well above average" in leadership ability; twenty-five percent reported themselves "below average." However, in "ability to get along with others," no one out of 830,000 rated themselves as below average. Sixty percent rated themselves in the top ten percent, and twenty-five percent saw themselves in the top one percent. It gets a little crowded at the top.

In another survey conducted several years ago, ninety-four percent of randomly selected college faculty stated they were brighter than their average colleague. In a survey of automobile drivers, most drivers surveyed believed themselves to be more skillful than the average driver. Interestingly enough, most drivers who were hospitalized because of injuries sustained in traffic accidents considered themselves more skillful than the average driver.

The second reason to be concerned with pride is that it lets us off the hook too easily. If we place ourselves and our own vested interests at the center of our world, then whatever is comfortable for us is what we will do. This seems reasonable enough, at first blush, except that deep down we all know we have commitments and obligations to other people. It cannot be possible that if we always serve what is comfortable for us, then we will continue to do the right thing by people who depend upon us to honor our commitments — be they comfortable or uncomfortable.

Years ago, I learned about a desktop calendar that was really a parody of the self-esteem movement. It was called "Deep Thoughts" by Jack Handy. On one page it read, "The first thing I learned was to forgive myself. Then I told myself, 'Go ahead and do whatever you want. It's okay by me.'" That comes all too close to the way decisions are made today.

The third problem with pride is that it blinds us to what humility really means, and humility is the foundation of a happier life. We tend to think that someone who is humble has a poor self-image, but the truth is quite the opposite. Humility recognizes that we have been given some gifts, but we have not been given all of them. There are some things each of us does well, but there are other things we do not do so well. There are limits we cannot reach. There are tasks we cannot perform as well as others. In so many areas of our lives, we fall short of our own perfectionism just as we excel in other areas. It is the same for everyone. Others envy our skills as we envy theirs. Humility helps us to recognize our need for others.

In truth, humanity has been given a rich assortment of gifts of which you and I have received only a few. We could – if driven by pride – behave as if we had received all or most of those gifts. This would take a lot of pretending, because it simply isn't and cannot ever be true. So driven, we would resent any hint that someone else had more of these gifts than we do. We would hate the energy it takes to pretend, and our resentment would turn to disdain for those who do not pretend to have gifts they know they do not have.

It is healthier to be enormously grateful that other people have gifts we do not have. For example, I am so glad that other people can make sense of a musical score and translate it into sound that I can enjoy. I cannot do this for myself. All of the skills other people have make my life richer, because I do not have to have or pretend that I have those skills. They exist for me as gifts from the rest of the world. Understanding that the world is ready to give gifts to us signals an important change in anyone's religious thinking.

Once a psychiatrist was seeing two patients, a lawyer and a doctor. They did not know each other. Each had sought help after realizing that he was generally disliked by just about everyone who knew him. The problem for each seemed to be arrogance.

As part of their therapy, the lawyer was assigned to read and report on several articles from the *New England Journal of Medicine*, and the doctor was asked to comment on several articles in the *Harvard Law Review*. It didn't take long for each to realize that outside of his own specific skills, he was completely indebted to the training, insights, and native ability of other people. Not only that, but the idea began to grow in each that he was indebted to a world of people who understood things he could not comprehend. As each man recognized the gifts that came into his life from sources other than himself, he learned to recognize, welcome, and feel grateful for the many gifts of life.

May we cease trying to hold our worlds together single-handedly. May we learn to play our parts in a wide world of many gifts, most of which will come to us from others. May we learn the higher commitments to one another that make living in this world not only possible but also even enjoyable.

There may be moments when we are tempted or goaded to pretend that we can storm the gates of heaven and come away with all of the wisdom that men and women can possess, but that would be a terribly unsatisfying life. Our lives are blessed by a creative mystery that distributes gifts broadly but in a way that always exceeds the bounds of our understanding.

CHAPTER 4

Why is Joseph in the Bible?

The book of Genesis has been, so far, a story of patriarchs seeking to have their own way and God leaning on the scale of justice however it might suit him. Yet in the lead-up to the story of Joseph and throughout it, we find a creative mystery that works through dreams and subtle promptings along the way.

If you had to pick a goal for the rest of your life, would you choose to do well, or would you choose to do good? When we choose to do well, we take every possible advantage. We defeat every conceivable competitor. In order to do well, we must never lose sight of how we would personally benefit from any decision or any turn of events. There may be good deeds we can do easily along the way or generous acts that wouldn't cost us all that much, but at the end of the day we need to keep our eyes on the prize that we hope to win for ourselves. That's what it means to do well.

When we choose to do good, we look with a different angle of vision — one that includes other people and their needs. If we choose to do good, we will make our choices conform to standards of justice, fairness, kindness, and compassion for the people around us. When we do well, we are guided by our dreams of individual success and personal security. When we do good, our dream is of being an important part of a community, a nation, or a world that is in harmony.

So, would you choose to do well, or would you choose to do good? It is not an easy choice. The truth is that we live in both worlds — the pragmatic and the idealistic. We need to do well, because there are people who depend upon us to do well. We would also like to do good, because our idealized image of ourselves is that we ought to be able to do good. We are often pulled in two directions: wanting to do well for ourselves and wanting to do good for others. Equally as often, we recognize that we do not test ourselves nearly enough.

There are times when our society seems to tilt in the direction of competitiveness and acquisition. The people live in only one, very well-defined world where doing good is quaint, out of step, and impossibly unrealistic. It was in and for just such a time that the story of Joseph was written to counteract the dominant themes of that acquisitive world.

Many scholars believe that the story of Joseph was written during the reigns of David and Solomon. Israel had become a great kingdom. Many people were doing extraordinarily well, and they could afford to fill large houses with fine things and enough servants to make life very easy. In their newfound fortresses of security and finery, many people became embarrassed by the religion of their ancestors. Who needed this stuffy God with his unyielding commandments? Who needed this petulant God with his fists full of thunderbolts? Who had thought up this God anyway? Why should they be asked to be loyal to a religion so remote from their own vested interests?

The ancient legends were not working for them — the legends that included the God who spoke to Abraham and caused him to go on a pilgrimage; the God who threatened to destroy Sodom and Gomorrah; the God who demanded the sacrifice of Isaac; and even the God who led the Israelites out of Egypt. Old stuff. It is quite possible that in the time when the story of Joseph was written, many no longer believed in God, in miracles, or for that matter, in doing good for other people.

Their religious leaders wondered how to convey the inexplicable, the sacredness that is wrapped in mystery, the value of doing good at a time when it is so much easier to understand the value of taking care of number one. As people have asked in every age, what is the use of doing good when God does not seem to punish people who live purely to do well for themselves?

Through the stories of Jacob and Joseph, the religious leaders of David and Solomon's kingdom tried to make it clear that the impulse for doing good does not require fear of blustery old Yahweh, stomping around heaven. They knew this ancient idea of God neither terrified nor impressed the people they served. Instead, the storytellers described a force for good that worked quietly through the visions and even the dreams of very ordinary and even difficult people. This force for good becomes a power to which we yield simply because it brings out what we know is the best in all of us. The stories of both Jacob and Joseph are in the Bible to demonstrate this point.

Joseph's family is the key to what Joseph became. His grandfather Isaac was the child that Abraham obediently tried to sacrifice, because he thought God wanted it that way. Apparently, Isaac was so traumatized by the experience that he never became a real person in his own right. But when he was old and nearly blind, his two sons Jacob and Esau competed with one another for the blessing of their witless elderly father.

In order to steal this blessing, Jacob connived with his mother to trick his father and cheat his brother. A lot of good it did him. Esau was so angry that Jacob had fooled their father and stolen his blessing that Jacob had to flee to another country.

While there, he met and fell in love with Rachel. Her father, Laban, told Jacob he could marry Rachel if he put in seven years of labor on the family ranch. He agreed. However, seven years later, on the morning after the wedding, the veiled woman he had married the night before turned out to be Rachel's older sister Leah. It was possibly the first "bait and switch" in the history of humankind. Laban responded to Jacob's fury saying, "Oh well, that's just the way we do things around here. But after another seven years of hard work, you can also marry Rachel."

So, Jacob had tricked his father, cheated his brother, and in turn was cheated by his father-in-law. A great deal of cheating followed on both sides. Eventually, Jacob was allowed to marry Rachel and to continue to work for Laban. But it became clear to Jacob that Laban resented his success as a businessman. One night, Jacob conspired with his wives and servants to flee, taking with him the better part of Laban's flocks and other goods.

Now, Jacob had no place to go but home. He well remembered that his brother Esau had promised to kill him if he ever returned there. When Jacob's group reached the broad river that bordered the land of Esau, they discovered that Esau had arrayed his entire clan on the other side. Ever the manipulator, Jacob decided that he should send his wives and slaves to cross the river ahead of him and see if that didn't soften old Esau up. Alone, Jacob lay down on the safe side of the river for the night.

According to the story, a stranger showed up that night and engaged Jacob in a wrestling match. This is not the usual thing that happens in Bible stories, so we have to ask why. Who was the stranger, and why was this stranger in our story? It seems clear that the stranger has some kind of symbolic importance. The story tells us that Jacob and the stranger wrestled all night, and neither could gain an advantage over the other. Finally,

Jacob said to the stranger, "I will not let you go until you bless me."

The stranger asked, "What is your name?" He was, in effect, asking "Who are you really? What do you stand for? What are your values?" After Jacob responded to the stranger, the stranger replied, "I will give you a new name." And he called Jacob "Israel," which some texts translate as, "He struggles with God."

We traditionally interpret that the stranger Jacob wrestled with had to be God. It makes as much sense, if not more, for us to believe that Jacob wrestled with his conscience. In the end, he did not overpower the stranger, though he could have. Jacob could always beat his conscience. What he did in this instance was give in to it. And the story tells us that even after Jacob had been released, he would walk with a limp for the rest of his life.

Jacob's conscience would be forever after a presence – sometimes a painful presence – in his life. He would always be reminded it was there, because he would always limp. Jacob — the liar, the cheat, the trickster, the man who always knew what it took to do well — had his life and his name changed, not by the fear of God but by grudging respect for God who from this point on would be a force in the back of his mind that must always be reckoned with.

The next morning, as it had turned out, Esau could not sustain the rage he originally felt, and so the brothers were tearfully reunited. They pledged to lead different lives. For the most part, they did – with occasional lapses in good conduct.

As the story of Joseph begins, Jacob is an old man. He has twelve sons. Six are sons also of Leah, the woman who tricked him. Two are sons of Leah's maid. Two are sons of Rachel's maid. Two are sons he shared with his beloved Rachel; those two are Joseph and Benjamin. At the beginning of the story, it becomes clear that sibling rivalry runs deep among the sons of

Jacob, as it did between Jacob and his brother Esau and as it does in most families.

Joseph is clearly the beloved son, and he knows it. He conducts himself in ways that are guaranteed to antagonize his brothers. They respond predictably, except that their anger toward Joseph is so great that they throw him into a pit and then contrive to sell him into slavery. They smear his clothing with goat's blood and proceed to deceive their father.

But Joseph survives. He becomes, in effect, the Egyptian pharaoh's secretary of the interior. When famine strikes, the entire world comes to Joseph for some of the grain that he has wisely saved against that possibility. Even Joseph's brothers must come to him for food though they do not know who he is.

Which Joseph will they find? Will they find Joseph the son of Jacob who determined for much of his life to do well? Or will they find the son of Jacob who had wrestled with his conscience and afterwards tried to remember that he was dedicated to something better than merely doing well? Not surprisingly, Joseph responds initially as the cynical world would have expected him to respond. He responds as a man of his time, his place, and his culture would respond. He also responds as the despised and rejected younger brother would respond — perhaps as many of us would respond.

Joseph plays with his brothers as a cat would play with a mouse. He tests them. He puts them in jail. He sends them away but plants stolen property in their luggage that he sends his guards to "discover" so that they can bring the brothers back to be accused now as thieves. Finally, he leans on them to go home and return with his full brother Benjamin, the other son of Rachel. Then he announces he will keep Benjamin with him.

At this point, his older brother Judah speaks the words that begin the final reconciliation. Filled with remorse for the grief of his father – the father who had rejected him and most of his siblings – Judah spoke of the guilt he shared with his brothers and pleaded for understanding. At the same time, Joseph suddenly loses his taste for vengeance, reveals who he is, and begins the process that will make it possible for the entire family to be united.

Father and sons reunite — really an amazing thing considering the state of families and rivalries in those days. Jacob lived to see his sons do good, even though God knows, they had experimented in all kinds of ways with merely doing well. Even at the end, when Jacob died, the brothers wondered if Joseph would now feel freer to retaliate against them. Joseph reassured them saying, "Don't be afraid. Am I in the place of God? You intended to harm me, but God intended it for good to save many lives."

So why is the Joseph story in the Bible? If you look carefully at the stories of Genesis, you begin to wonder why any of those characters is being held up to us as a patriarch. Abraham, Sarah, Isaac, Jacob, Esau, Joseph, and his brothers are all very limited human beings. They have all of the traits and passions that get us into trouble. They lie, cheat, steal, and attempt to dominate one another. The only one of them you'd even think of inviting over for wine and cheese would be Joseph, and after twenty minutes he would have told you so much about himself that you'd wish he never came.

Some time ago, a Biblical scholar wrote a book suggesting that these stories may actually have been written by a woman, reflecting on the idiotic ways of men – their conceits, their vanities, and their blindness. It's not a widely held theory. Even if it were true, why would the men who compiled the Bible cannon have included these stories at all? Here, I think, is the reason.

The people who compiled the Bible cannon saw the human condition just as clearly and distressingly as we see it today. But they also saw our ability to wrestle with a conscience and give ourselves to it as willingly as Jacob did. They saw that, incredibly, we can also connect with the hopes, dreams, fears, as well as the humanity of other people. In making that connection, we can get beyond the barriers that keep us separated, as Joseph finally did. There are folks who believe the Bible is about war. I think it is more accurate to say it is about reconciliation.

If there is a dream to celebrate in the Joseph story, it is a dream of reconciliation. It is the dream we acknowledge at Thanksgiving. It is the dream that haunts our Christmas carols. It is both a dream and a conviction that the force we each wrestle and yield to sometimes is pulling us toward a gentler life together. It is admittedly a fragile dream, but it is also the only thing that has enabled us to believe that a world without continuous fratricide is possible.

CHAPTER 5

The Ten Commandments

The Ten Commandments found in Exodus 20 and Deuteronomy 10 have such a history of development and interpretation that whole books have been written on them — when the commandments were first conceived and how they spoke to the culture for which they were written. This chapter presents an attempt to understand the Ten Commandments in relation to the lives we live now. Quite different interpretations can be found online or in the library.

The ground literally shook. Lightening lit up the sky. The thunder was so loud that people searched for some place to hide. Something terrible and awesome was about to happen. This is how the scene is set for the appearance of the Ten Commandments.

We take them for granted now, or they have become just another symbol for religious liberals and conservatives to fight over. We joke about amending them into the "Ten Suggestions." To many, they seem like something primitive and quaint out of a past that has little to teach us. I am sure that even those who advocate posting the Ten Commandments in courtrooms and school buildings think of them as a bunch of ancient prohibitions – a list of "Thou Shalt Nots."

I firmly believe, however, that ancient people may have been ancient, but they weren't stupid. If they felt something was terribly important, they may have had good reason to feel that way, and we should take them seriously. A powerful idea lies at the core of these commandments, an idea that is not – as most people presume – a prohibition. Instead, it is a permission. The Ten Commandments give permission that we vitally need to take ourselves, our life, and the lives of others more seriously.

Let's revisit the Ten Commandments, but this time not as children listening to them in church school. We'll take the text as text and not worry about whether it is history. Let's talk about it as adults who have lived a while and now know some of the traps into which adults can fall.

To set the scene, the sky darkens. The ground shakes. Something important must be about to happen. Then out of the thundercloud, a voice speaks. It is God speaking to Moses. However, God's self-description is the key to what the story means. First listen to what God does *not* say to describe who God is.

God does *not* say, "I am the creator of heaven and earth." God does *not* say, "I am more powerful than you can believe." God does *not* say, "I am smarter than every last one of you suckers." God *does* say, "I am the Lord your God who brought you out of the land of Egypt, out of the house of slavery." God's self-description is, "I gave you freedom." The Ten Commandments are a testament to freedom today as much as when they were issued. Freedom is the point.

For example, "Honor your father and your mother so that your days may be long in the land that God is giving you." This is one of the commandments to which, right away, some will respond, "Well, I don't know about that!" People who have complex relationships with their parents may hear this as offering them even more grief and guilt. Unpacking troubled childhoods has been the substance of many novels and much therapy, so honoring parents may not necessarily sound like an idea in harmony with your mental health. But it is.

Listen again very carefully to what that commandment does *not* say. It does *not* say, "Listen to your father and mother and do everything they ask of you." It does *not* say, "Copy your father and mother because you can't possibly improve on them." It does *not* say that we should be prepared to feel incredibly guilty every time one of our parents gets a little bit cranky. It does *not* even say that we should love our parents, because love is something that cannot be forced. It says that we should *honor* our parents.

What does that mean, and what does it have to do with freedom? When we honor our parents, we recognize that they are the people who gave us a portion of their lives so that we could become independent adults. We honor that gift best by remaining independent adults, capable of appreciating the people who sheltered, clothed, fed, taught, and — to the best of their ability — loved us. But we must also be capable of knowing where our parents' lives stop and our own lives must begin.

The first step in honoring our parents is recognizing that being limited and fallible people, they did the best they could in a role for which almost nobody is a natural, and few are even very well prepared. I am sure almost everyone wishes his or her parents had done something differently. I am sure there are times when most parents wish they had done something differently. The gap between what we believe we ought to do and what we finally accomplish will always be wide. Thank God it is, or we would be willing to settle for giving too little of ourselves.

The commandment goes even further. It asks us to honor our parents so that we can live a long and useful life. How is a long life related to respecting one's parents? Here, the deeper meaning of this commandment – and of all the commandments – deals with the freedom each of us needs to develop as people. When I speak about freedom, I am not just speaking about freedom from known tyrants. I am speaking particularly about freedom from tyrannies that we create to enslave ourselves.

If honoring our fathers and mothers means accepting that they are people to whom we owe respect, consideration, and a measure of care – regardless of our history with them, then it also means accepting that they and we are independent individuals. There is a point at which their lives and our lives have boundaries that do not overlap. Whatever we may regret from our childhood, it is our responsibility to live now so we do not pass our own injuries along and so that our regrets plague us less and less.

We can freely live the rest of our lives without being haunted either by the mistakes we now believe they made when raising us or by the guilt that often lasts long after an adult-to-child relationship should have become adult-to-adult. Our parents need to live without that guilt as well. When the independence of parent from child and of child from parent is established, then the days of each can be longer and happier on the earth. Children watching how their parents treat their grandparents will learn how respect links the generations by honoring both their togetherness and their separateness.

Among God's first words from out of the thundercloud are, "You shall have no other gods before me," and "You shall not make for yourself an idol." In the ancient Middle East, there were a multitude of gods and some goddesses; most were approached through the worship of idols. But the Jews had already observed that many people are all too happy to use the worship of idols as an excuse to rid themselves of the burden of making the choices that free adults must make.

Looking back on the time when they had been enslaved to Egyptian idols, the Jews remembered that they had been very comfortable being slaves. As slaves, they had shelter, meals, security, laws, government, and a sense of identity provided for them. They missed all of that when they lived in freedom. They came to long for security, long for it enough to consider seriously giving up the freedom to shape their own lives. Even as the stone tablets were being given on Sinai, the folks down below were constructing an idol to inspire them with courage, because they didn't think they could find their own courage and purpose for living.

At a deeper level, the storyteller also understood that we create personal idols all the time. Then we hope that our idols will work magic to bring us happiness and security. One individual might pour his life's energies into building and furnishing a new house, believing and hoping that this house will eventually provide the comfort that is missing from his life.

Another may idolize reaching a level of personal or professional success, hoping that this recognition, once achieved, will repay the energy and the dreams that have been poured into earning it. Some parents may idolize a child – not the real child, of course – but a vision of what that child may accomplish someday and the ways in which that accomplishment will bring happiness and due reward back to his or her parents.

"You shall not make for yourself an idol" becomes a commandment not because the God in this story cannot stand some folks lighting incense in front of their home altars. Rather, this God who wants us to have the full blessings of freedom warns us not to give up our chance for real happiness by investing our hopes in the false security of something we create only to flatter ourselves. "You shall have no other gods before me" means taking responsibility for the person you will become. Use the freedom you have been given. Do not invest your hopes in something that will only draw you farther away from the choices only you can and must make.

Another commandment tells us, "You shall not make wrongful use of the name of the Lord." We know this as "not taking the Lord's name in vain." This is not, as most people think, merely a prohibition against saying "God damn it" when "Goll darn it" would do. This commandment wants us to stand on our own two feet as free individuals and take responsibility for what we believe, for what we support, for what we oppose, and for the honesty of our speech without dragging in God to vouch for us.

For example, when someone says, "I swear to God I'm telling the truth," the point of the commandment is, "Do not presume to know what God would or would not say about the quality of your truthfulness. Let your honesty stand on its own so that no one will ever doubt it." Don't drag God into your speech, either to make yourself sound grander than you are by proclaiming that God blesses your particular religion or politics or by suggesting that you and God are good buddies who will never have a falling out. Don't hide your views, your decisions, and your commitments behind God. It was not for that purpose that God promised to free you even from the slaveries you create to enslave yourself.

"Remember the Sabbath and keep it holy." During the years the Hebrew people spent in slavery, there was no Sabbath. Men and women worked as long as their masters wanted them to work. They were valued only because they produced what other people wanted, not because of what they thought, felt, or expressed. They were not valued because they were wise, funny, creative, or courageous but because their work brought forth a product.

When they were released from slavery, the Hebrew people asked themselves, "How will we ever know if we start slipping back into devising our own, even more clever forms of personal captivity? How will we know when we have quietly started giving back our freedoms to love the people we love, to care for other people who care for us, and to serve our deepest convictions? How will we know, before it is too late, that we are no longer allowing ourselves the time to entertain dreams that matter or to raise children who will have their own dreams? How will we know when all of this begins to slip slide away from us?"

From somewhere, they conceived the story that even God rested after six days of work. So, who are we to think that our work is so much more important than God's work that it demands our continual attention with no rest? Remember the Sabbath and keep it holy. If you do not, you will work relentlessly either to serve someone else's needs or to appease your own personal idols. Either way, you've lost your freedom. Shortly after losing your freedom, you lose much of the pleasure you take in living. Who finally commands the time in your life if not you?

A couple of years ago while out walking, I tripped and pitched forward toward the pavement. I thrust my arm out in order to stop my fall, and I injured it. For a while I minimized the extent of the injury. However, when the pain and swelling would not go away, I went to the doctor. When he suggested I would probably need a cast on both my hand and my arm, I balked. That would interfere with both my driving and my ability to write, for example, a sermon. He said, "It's up to you. This is your arm. It is the only human arm God is giving you. You will not get another. You are responsible for how you take care of it." That made an impression on me.

In presenting the Ten Commandments, the God of this story is saying, "This is your life. It is the only life I am giving you. Here is your freedom. Take good care to nurture it, or you will lose it. There will be many ways in which you will be tempted to ignore that freedom or even diminish the gift of life itself. There will be temptations. If you yield even to one of them, you will very likely yield to more than one. Then you will unwittingly give your freedom away."

God continues, "You shall not murder, because each life is my gift to someone that you are not entitled to take away. You shall not bear false witness against someone else, because you dishonor yourself with a lie as much as you mislead others. You shall not commit adultery, because it is a lie; it is being false to yourself as well as to others. You shall not covet or steal, because then you encroach upon the life and freedom of another individual."

We don't really know under what actual circumstances the Ten Commandments came together into one passage. But we do know that the storyteller went to some lengths to be sure we understood that this was an important moment. He describes the ground shaking, accompanied by thunder and lightning. Most people now assume this means that old Father God was intending to put a scare into the kids.

In this story, God is trying to get everyone's attention but not scare them. God is giving permission: "I have given you life and freedom. Use it well. Do not misuse it. And respect always the life and freedom I have given to others. Do these things, and you will live long and well."

CHAPTER 6

Remembering Jonah

We don't laugh at the story of Jonah because it's in the Bible. But maybe we should laugh at it, just as we laugh at other traits we see in ourselves and others, so that we can accept that they are real. And we all know it.

The ancient story of Jonah comes from a land where violence is a frequent visitor. We value the story of Jonah not just because it is ancient, but also because it reflects what men and women who sought to find a better way of living have affirmed over centuries of wars, retributions, and political chicaneries. This story is about what others have learned from their mistakes, from their blindness, and from the suffering that comes from that blindness. That is why Jonah is one of the texts used in synagogues during the Jewish High Holy Days.

In some ways, Jonah is a silly story. It has a comic element, which I will exploit shamelessly. It is also a serious story, because it reminds us both of the devices and desires of our own hearts and of the causes of hatred and violence that we find within us and within everyone. We have all heard something about Jonah. But be aware; I am going to dress it in contemporary garb. It will sound a little differently. You might think you know where the story is going to come out, but you might be wrong.

Jonah was an average sort of guy. He worked hard all year and looked forward to spending two weeks with his family in their timeshare condominium by the Dead Sea. But one day — just a week before his vacation — God came to Jonah and said, "Go and warn the people of Nineveh that they are doing bad things. If they don't clean up their act, I am going to punish the whole misbegotten lot of them."

Now why did God pick Jonah for this difficult and onerous task? Jonah wasn't a diplomat or a clergyman. He was just an average "Jonah" who had been looking forward to a couple of weeks with the family by the Dead Sea — maybe some beach volleyball, some cookouts, kosher franks, maybe a whale watch, the whole ball of wax. But we find out from other stories that the God character in this story has a habit of asking people for a level of courage or commitment they think they cannot achieve and then do. It's now Jonah's turn to be tested.

It seems that God does know the assignment of calling the Ninevites to repent will be difficult for Jonah. God knows Jonah hates the people of Nineveh. He hates them as much as any ethnic group could hate another. The Ninevites are not of his people. They are not of his religion. They are not easy to get along with. The last time Jonah's softball team played the Ninevite Nine, the pitcher struck him out four times. After the last strikeout, the pitcher did a little victory dance to enhance Jonah's humiliation.

So, if the people of Nineveh were doing something that would get them into trouble with God, Jonah thought that would be just fine and dandy. If the people of Nineveh could be visited by divine wrath — and thoroughly whacked for their sins — well that was just lovely with Jonah. He does not trust this old softie God to seek fairness in the way Jonah thinks fairness should be sought.

In Jonah's world, "fairness" means "I want what's mine, and if anyone offends me, I want them slapped around at the very least." This character God is all too inclined to give people another chance. Jonah wants no part of that. Fair is fair, and Jonah thinks he knows what fair is. Jonah thinks he knows better than God what fair is. Jonah thinks that "fair" means "it's payback time for Nineveh."

So, Jonah defies God. Rather than participate in any mission of reconciliation, Jonah books passage on a ship going away from Nineveh in the hopes that God will forget about having asked him to save the people of Nineveh. But the ship gets caught in a storm. The sailors, who are not of Jonah's religion, are convinced that someone on board is on the "outs" with his God. So they draw straws hoping that fate will determine which person it is and whose god they should attempt to appease to stop the sea from rolling.

Meanwhile, Jonah is asleep in the bottom of the boat because he doesn't particularly care what danger he has put everyone in. The sailors conclude that it is Jonah who has put them in this peril. When confronted, Jonah admits that, well, yes, his God probably is angry with him and that probably has caused the storm. But no, Jonah will not pray to his God and ask that God to forgive him, because Jonah thinks he knows better than God what is fair and that the Ninevites deserve to be punished rather than saved.

Rather than give up the notion that his idea of justice should be imposed on the universe, Jonah will take the whole ship down with him. But then he relents and tells the sailors, "Look if you want to stop the storm, just throw me over the side of the ship and the storm will stop."

The sailors don't want to throw Jonah overboard. The storyteller is making the point that these essentially pagan sailors are made of more compassionate stuff than the self-righteous, deeply pious, pillar of religion Jonah. At great risk to their own lives, the sailors get into smaller boats and try to row the ship into calmer waters. But Jonah doesn't care whether he lives or dies or who dies trying to save his life. He would rather drown than change his fixation on what he thinks life owes him.

Finally, having no other choice, the crew members do toss Jonah over the side. And the seas do become calm. Jonah is then swallowed into the belly of a big fish where he stays for three days. Now it would be hard for any of us to imagine what he did in the belly of a fish for three days. He had no cell phone, no television, and no video games. He couldn't receive email. The text tells us that Jonah wrote a poem.

God had rescued Jonah – though he didn't deserve it – but Jonah goes on and on in this poem about what a great guy Jonah is, what a great friend God is, and what a close relationship they are going to have now that Jonah has been saved. Apparently, the fish is so disgusted with this self-righteous drivel that it goes, "Yuck!" According to the text, the fish "vomited" Jonah up onto dry land.

Jonah is not out of the storm. The text wants us to know that the real storm is inside of Jonah. He is drunk on the idea of his own goodness. He is so tossed and turned by his sense of the injustices he thinks ought to be made right to him that he has lost all track of other people – how they feel or what they want. He doesn't know or care if they exist. The only thing that matters to him is that someone should settle the scores Jonah believes need to be settled in order that things will seem fair to Jonah. If that won't happen, he doesn't much care what else does happen.

God isn't impressed with Jonah's change of heart. However, God does send him back to Nineveh to warn them that if they do not stop doing evil things, they will be punished. Not wanting to become fish food again, this time Jonah goes. But the text tells us that he never went much beyond the outskirts of the city.

Jonah's mission is half-hearted, to say the least. He barely walks into the city. Then, thinking there is no one around, he says in a soft quiet voice, "Uh, you people wouldn't believe that God is going to punish you if you don't stop sinning? Nah, I didn't think so. Probably just a miscommunication. That's all right. Just pay no attention to me. Just go right on sinning. Don't let me stop you. I'll just go up on that hill and take a rest."

Hoping that he had been a spectacular failure at prophecy and social reform, Jonah retired to the hillside to watch the fun. But incredibly, someone in Nineveh heard him, believed him, and went to the king, who also believed him and proclaimed a national day of repentance. The God character in this story is so touched that the city is spared.

But Jonah is furious. He says to God, "Now you see. I knew this would happen. Where is the justice here, God? Where is the fairness? You went soft on me. I've been waiting here for forty days and forty nights to watch Nineveh get what it richly deserves, and nothing has happened." Jonah was in a very bad mood. The sun was beating down on him, and he was angry.

God causes a large plant to grow over Jonah, and it gives him so much shade that he begins to feel better about life and about himself. "Perhaps," Jonah thinks, "all is not lost. Perhaps there is goodness in the world." Just when Jonah was feeling good about himself, God then caused the plant to wither and die, leaving Jonah sweltering in the hot sun again. Jonah became boiling mad.

God then speaks to Jonah, "Are you angry?" Jonah says, "Are you kidding? I am so angry that I want to die, again." Then the character God said something like, "Think about it, Jonah. You did not make this plant. It was one of life's good gifts to you. But you were sorry for its death only because it ceased to be of use to you. Yet you felt nothing at all for the lives of 120,000 people who were not of your family, tribe, or religion."

Interestingly enough, the story ends here. We don't know if Jonah got the point or if his mind had been changed in any way. This may be the storyteller's way of saying that the battle against self-righteousness never really ends. It never ends in the life of a nation. It never really ends in the life of a community. And it never really ends in your life or mine. The temptation to judge other people harshly is always there, even when we think we've licked it.

The most obvious message of this story is that self-righteousness is the curse of humankind in every part of the world. It is not — as it claims to be — on the side of virtue, protecting only the good people in the world. It is the enemy of life. Whenever a self-righteous attitude dismisses the wonder and complexity of any living person or people, then there is an attitude that harms all life and defeats itself. Ultimately self-righteousness defeats itself.

One part of the Jonah story has to do with self-righteousness, but another aspect has to do with fairness. Jonah didn't think it was fair that the Ninevites got off so easily after all their sinning. We can side with that feeling. There are many things that do seem inherently unfair. Nasty and cruel people enjoy perfect health while people who are kind and generous get struck down in the prime of their lives. It's not fair.

It's not fair that some parents must bury their child. It is not fair that some people are born advantaged and others disadvantaged simply by the way families and genes sort themselves out. It's not fair that some people struggle to achieve what comes easily to others. It is not fair that people die, because they are accidentally in the wrong place at the wrong time.

We have believed in fairness since we learned it as children. It is difficult for us to realize that there may just be an aching inequality in life itself. The playing field is never entirely level.

Fairness — if it means that equal measures of good and bad luck, success and failure come to every individual — is not life's issue. I do not think that fairness is God's issue either. I'm not sure that God can make everything fair, but I am sure that eye-for-eye fairness is neither what God nor life intends.

In the story, Jonah tells God, "This isn't fair. You should punish those people." God responds, in effect, "Jonah, it's not about fairness. It's about compassion." What the story conveys is that we cannot make right all the hard things that happen to people, and we may not even be able to correct some of the most grievous wrongs. However, we can be a force of compassion in the world. We can be part of the work of reconciliation in this world.

The Jewish High Holy Days or the beginning of a new Unitarian Universalist worship year — they usually coalesce around the same time — asks us this question: What kind of person are you going to be in this new year? Are you going to expend precious energy bemoaning that life has not dealt you what you think you deserve? Are you going to drag old grievances into the new year, burdening yourself and boring everybody else? Will you be part of a Greek chorus, lamenting what we already know — that the good things in life have not fallen equally upon all of us? Or will you be a source of courage, healing, and hope for others? It's a choice that each of us has to make.

Finally, if life is not fair, what is there to celebrate? Certainly not that we are all alone on this darkling plane where anything could happen, and nobody cares. If we have learned anything meaningful from living, and if we have been open to being taught, perhaps it is this: While we live, we still have more blessings than we can or ever will appreciate. Life offers us more forgiveness than we think we deserve and more power than we can call upon to change things for the good of others.

Life surrounds us with people who would support us if we allowed them and with opportunities that would challenge and change us if we accepted that challenge. Fairness is not life's issue. And I don't think it is God's issue. Life's issue with us, or as some might say, God's issue, is that we fully accept the gifts we have been given and make the best use of them so that we become agents of the world's kindness and compassion.

CHAPTER 7

The Challenges of Job

We often hear of the patience of Job, but the truth is that Job was not a patient man. He had been a pillar of the community; then, his life was ruined. The book of Job is about what works and what doesn't work when an individual reaches the depths of despair. The happy ending, which is not part of the original author's intent, obscures the fact that the real question of the story is left open for each of us to answer.

Because I grew up in the atmosphere of the liberal Yale University community, I never had to defend being a Unitarian Universalist. Instead, I had to defend being religious at all. But then, going to Dickinson College in southcentral Pennsylvania was another matter. There I had to defend being liberally religious. We didn't spend all that much time discussing theology at Dickinson. In those years, the more typical male freshman topics were getting drunk, throwing up, and telling wild, bald-faced lies about our sexual prowess.

But, these were the early sixties, and religion was still an important topic to most people, including young adults. So it came up, and I couldn't keep quiet. I discovered that most of my classmates had never met anyone like me. They had never met someone who *did not* believe in eternal punishment for sin. As they saw it, if you don't believe that God's going to make you pay for what you've done wrong – now or in the life hereafter – then you have no reason to be good and every reason to try and get away with whatever you can.

No one actually questioned that I was a moral person – at least by the standards of college freshmen, which were pretty low after all. But since I did not believe in a punishing God, they just couldn't figure out what would keep me moral. Or perhaps they couldn't figure out why I wasn't having more fun breaking the rules.

A girlfriend who had known me for two years finally broke up our relationship because, she said, she could not be in love with someone who did not believe in a God of punishment. As I thought about that in writing this sermon, I realized that her statement is probably unique in the realm of excuses given for breaking up a relationship. She later married a devout Episcopalian named Alpha Omega, which gave me a clue as to what she had been seeking.

At the time, I didn't realize that punishment is the question that has haunted the Western world for the last several hundred years. If there is no Divine punishment, we ought to be able to get away with anything. If God isn't policing the playground or at least taking notes, why isn't everything possible or permissible for the crooks and bullies of the world?

It is not an unreasonable question, and we ask it because we all know the devices and desires of our own hearts. We know there are corners we have been tempted to cut and people we've been tempted to cheat or betray. There have been good opportunities we could have taken if we had overlooked just a few scruples.

What would happen if everything that props up what we believe is goodness was taken away, and every community became a place where might makes right? This is *the question* that is asked in the book of Job. I hope you remember it, at least vaguely. Everything Job has ever cherished is taken away from him. There is no reason for this punishment — if it is a punishment. We wonder what it is that Job has left to gain from remaining a moral and upright individual.

I will get back to Job in a minute, but first I want to look at a time in real history when almost all the props of society actually were taken away. How did people behave when they were left with very little faith that there was a comprehensible morality operating in the world? What if most people believed that everything was up for grabs? To try to answer that question, I want to go back to the fourteenth century in Europe.

Why? The Black Plague swept through Europe, killing somewhere between thirty-five to forty percent of the entire population. In urban areas, the toll was much more dramatic. For instance, one-third of all the people in Paris died in a very short period of time. This terrible illness was no respecter of age, gender, status, or moral condition. It swept through families, armies, governments, and churches. At times, there were hardly enough people strong enough to bury the dead or even to pray for them.

If the plague had come only once and gone away in each community, then people might still have believed that it was God's punishment for some specific sins. But the plague waxed and waned with the fate of the flea and rat population. Therefore, it never seemed to leave the community entirely. It kept coming back.

The prospect of the Black Death brooded constantly over a people who believed that what was happening violated any idea they may have had of a just God who rewarded the faithful with a good and long life. The Black Death changed forever the politics and the economics of Europe. It particularly changed the spiritual outlook in Europe.

The people decided that whatever God's will was or was not in this situation, the church obviously did not know it and could not help them. The people of fourteenth-century Europe decided that if the church could not save them, they had to find some way to save themselves or at least to make the best of what life they had left to them.

Remember that in that time, the people had no idea what was causing these deaths. Some decided that rich living was the cause of the sickness. These people chose to live in communes where only certain foods were allowed, and no sick people were permitted to enter. We have such enclaves today for people with nutritional and other health ideologies.

Others hoped to escape and hide, as far away from other people and from the sickness as possible, hoping that even God would never find them. Today we call this "circling the wagons." On the other hand, others said that since there seemed to be no way anyone could save himself, really, the best thing to do was to eat, drink, and be merry in the short time they had left before death finally reached them. This response to life is represented among contemporary Americans as well.

Prior to the Black Death, most people thought they were expected to do honest, hard work for their entire lives to get their reward. Now, it became clear that one could work hard all his life, and there was no guarantee that he might not face an agonizing early death. What we see in the literature from the plague years is an emphasis on wit, cleverness, guile, and trickery. There was an emphasis on irony. Does that sound familiar?

The people began to wonder if life wasn't perhaps like a card game that worked better for crafty minds than for honest hearts. Today, many people – particularly, I think, among the young – admire most those who have successfully manipulated the world to their own personal benefit.

In early medieval society, each community had been run on pretty much of a cooperative basis. Some of it was enforced by feudalism. Regardless of the reason, most people believed that they could depend on one another and that they needed to depend on one another. The Black Death destroyed any ideas of cooperative communities. Instead, there was a new emphasis on everyone for his or her own self.

The Renaissance began to grow out of this new emphasis on individualism. Unfortunately, so did the idea that salvation or happiness requires gaining more material wealth than most other people have. Today, we see this frequently in the attitude of companies, professional associations, and corporations toward their employees and the readiness of most employees to vest no real loyalty in anything but their own self-interest.

The influence of the Christian church, which had begun to decline before the Black Plague, continued its downward trend. Its preachers had been extolling the virtues of an all-powerful, personal God, but they could not explain why God had done this harm to his people or how God could be persuaded to undo it.

You would think that many would begin to abandon a religious faith that did not seem to protect them from harm. Actually, they did not abandon religion. Instead, they began seeking individual relationships to a mystical source or power that might help them more directly than traditional Christianity.

Some became interested in astrology, magic, or witchcraft. Those who remained within the Christian fold reshaped their religious beliefs to reflect a more personal relationship to the Divine. In a very similar way today, many people who have lost their traditional faith are trying to work out their own individual relationships with a source of meaning they cannot describe but are unwilling to abandon.

Other things happened as a result of the changes brought about after the Black Death. Life, generally, took on more violent, emotional overtones. Pessimism replaced optimism in art and literature. In time, both art and literature became more escapist and less concerned with realism. People at least perceived a general breakdown of law and order.

Why did I spend some part of last summer reading about the Black Plague?[1] Because it struck me how similar, in some ways, the people's loss of confidence – and their loss of faith – was to our own. These things don't happen overnight; they take decades. But the result is the same. What will we call the plagues that we have seen over the twentieth century into the twenty-first century: pessimism, cynicism, materialism, fascism, communism? Most importantly, how will we respond to a society that seems to have lost some of its faith?

We come back to the book of Job. As it begins, God says, "Look at my servant, Job. Did you ever see such an honest and faithful guy?" And the accusing angel says, "Let me take away a few of his playthings, and I can assure you he will not be so faithful." But even as he loses all he has, Job continues to be a moral individual.

So, the accusing angel visits Job with a plague. Surely when his body is covered with boils and sores and he has not a moment of peace left in his physical life, Job will curse the God whom he cannot possibly trust any longer. To make matters worse, several friends visit Job and tell him in various ways that he shouldn't mind having his life destroyed, because it is all for some mysterious, higher purpose. That should really drive him away from both religion and morality.

Job is given every reason to say, "The hell with it!" If life or God is going to punish me – though I have done nothing to deserve it – then I will have nothing more to do with these foolish beliefs. If my religion profits me nothing, I will put it away. I will pay no attention to it. Instead, I will go out and put a spear through my neighbor who secretly hates me, and I will do whatever it takes – bar none – to have as good a life as I can before I die. By every common-sense criteria, Job has the right to say that, just as people today wonder how one can be good without believing in a punishing God.

What is astonishing is that Job does none of this. To the end of the book, he maintains that he led a good life. He led the life he should have led. He is sure that he was not stupid to have treated people with kindness and compassion or to have gone out of his way to help the unfortunate. He was not wrong to be honest, fair, or generous.

Job's final plea is, "If only God will hear me, state his case against me, let me read his indictment. . . . I would justify the least of my actions; I would stand before him like a prince." Job's argument is that God or not God, he had done the right thing by his neighbors, his family, his community, and his conscience. He simply believes he should have gotten more credit for it.

Of course, in the story Job is saved from his crisis of faith. God is finally stirred to answer him and does. In essence, God responds, "Look at this world; look at this life I gave you. Look at everything that has sustained you down through the years. Could you have done that for yourself? Are you in charge of the seasons, the tides, or any of the rhythms that have made your life whole? Don't bother answering. We both know the answer. Sometimes you have to face up to and bear what you do not like."

In the end – in what many believe to be a contrived, happy ending – God restores everything Job had in his previous life and then some. Perhaps we can assume that a story this radical – a story sharply questioning traditional assumptions – had to have a happy ending or its sponsor never would have bought it for the Bible.

Perhaps the interesting part is wondering what would happen if the story ended without the voice of God from the whirlwind. Job has made an eloquent case before God that his suffering is undeserved and should stop. Nothing happens;

there is silence. What will Job do now? Go out and rob a convenience store? Put a spear through his troublesome neighbor? Cheat on his taxes? No. He wouldn't do any of that.

Here is my point. Everything in the story leads me to believe that if Job could not receive an answer from God, then he would create a mental standard of his own that would guide his life. He would live as he always had. He would not lie, cheat, or harm others. Whether this ethic of compassion and kindness was God – inexplicably, silently within Job – or whether it was just stubborn human refusal to be inhuman will never be known.

We know Job's response would not be everyone's response. Reflecting on what happened in Europe after the Black Death, it seems clear that many people are motivated by a thoroughgoing selfishness which is curbed only when they believe they are being watched. In the worst of circumstances, the miracle is that there have been communities of individuals and isolated individuals who, even if they were not sure of God, could imagine a higher standard of caring and could hold themselves to that standard. Civilization has depended upon such people, and it always will.

Shortly after World War II, Albert Camus wrote a short novel called *The Plague* in which he described many of the circumstances that occurred during the actual plague but also during Europe's more recent plague that had been fascism. In his story, he recognizes that the vast majority of men and women will run for their own protection under severe circumstances. But there is always a percentage that will not, and upon them rests any hope for the world. Here are Camus' words about the World War II conditions, which he describes as a plague:

> It is fear and silence and the spiritual isolation they cause that must be fought today. And it is sociability and the

universal intercommunication between people that must be defended. . . . There is no reason why some of us should not take on the job of keeping alive . . . a modest thoughtfulness, which, without pretending to solve everything, will constantly be prepared to give some meaning to everyday life.

. . . I have always held that, if he who bases his hopes on human nature is a fool, he who gives up in the face of circumstances is a coward.[2]

Perhaps we also need to gamble that our power to light the world with truth and goodness is stronger than our tendency to fall prey to anger and indifference.

NOTES

1. Research for this sermon comes principally from: Robert Gottfried, *The Black Death: Natural and Human Disaster in Medieval Europe* (New York: The Free Press, paperback edition, 1985).

2. The quote by Albert Camus is from his essay "Towards Dialogue," one of a series of his essays that appeared in November 1946 in *Combat*, the daily newspaper of the French Resistance, and later published in a collection of his essays in the book *Neither Victims nor Executioners: An Ethic Superior to Murder*, which is widely available.

CHAPTER 8

What We Learn
from the Prophets

Most of these chapters have been sermons adapted for this book; this chapter is different. I have never preached on the prophets, primarily because – with a couple of exceptions – they were a gloomy bunch, and that's not my style. However, they are extremely important to the development of Bible-based religion. This brief chapter will seek to explain why.

Someone who foretells the future with reasonable accuracy is often called a prophet. This person probably has a great deal of courage, wisdom, and enough self-assurance to withstand the reaction of his/her detractors. Since the prophets' severe judgments are sometimes difficult to read, they must have been extremely difficult to hear. Yet, I think those prophecies are included in the Bible partially because they unpack the evolving religious beliefs of the Hebrew people.

Through close readings of the prophets' texts and to some extent from Biblical archeology, scholars can conjecture approximately when each prophet lived, where, and what they felt they were up against. It's a life-long study in and of itself, and I will not attempt to go into it any more than necessary. What I will do is present several prophets and include for each a passage or two that lingers in Western imaginations and shapes our thinking even today.

AMOS

One of the earliest prophets, Amos preached around 760-750 BC. He was a herdsman who showed up during the time of King Jeroboam II. It was a prosperous time in the kingdom. As in many instances of sudden prosperity, the differences between the "haves" and the "have-nots" had widened considerably. As has happened before and since, many generations of wealthy people had assumed they must be doing something right by God or they wouldn't be wealthy. This is how Amos read the situation:

> Because they sell the righteous for silver,
> and the needy for a pair of sandals –
> they who trample the head of the poor into the dust of the earth,
> and push the afflicted out of the way;
> father and son go in to the same girl,
> so that my holy name is profaned. (Amos 2:6–8)

In his book *Don't Know Much about the Bible*, Kenneth Davis writes:

> Preaching in a time of relative wealth and political stability, Amos attacked the oppression of the poor by the rich, empty piety, and immoral religious practices – the "father and son going in to the same girl" may have referred to the continuing popularity of temple prostitutes. According to Amos, God despises sacrifices, festivals, and songs if they are not accompanied by ethical behavior, and he stressed personal responsibility. If the people did not mend their corrupt ways, Amos said they would be destroyed. It wasn't a

popular message, and Amos was banished from Israel by
Jeroboam because his words were so harsh.[1]

In Amos 5:21–24, we hear the voice of Amos:

> I hate, I despise your festivals,
> And I take no delight in your solemn assemblies.
> Even though you offer me your burnt offerings and grain
> offerings
> I will not accept them;
> and the offerings of well-being of your fatted animals
> I will not look upon.
> Take away from me the noise of your songs;
> I will not listen to the melody of your harps.
> But let justice roll down like waters,
> and righteousness like an ever-flowing stream.

Martin Luther King Jr. reminds us of these ancient words and
hopes in his speech at the March on Washington on August 28,
1963:

> We can never be satisfied as long as our children are stripped
> of their selfhood and robbed of their dignity by signs stating,
> "For whites only." We cannot be satisfied as long as a Negro
> in Mississippi cannot vote and a Negro in New York believes
> he has nothing for which to vote. No, no we are not satisfied,
> and we will not be satisfied until justice rolls down like
> waters, and righteousness like a mighty stream.[2]

King is not the only one to have found these words in Amos.
Periodically through the centuries, they leap up and inspire
generations of visionary social reformers. In fact, when I trained
ministerial interns I found that they were quite captivated by
the words of Amos that proclaimed what they felt was the true
purpose of religion and put the wealthy in their place. I often
responded, "Well, just remember that Amos changed nothing
and lost his job – not a good model for successful ministry."

HOSEA

Hosea was another matter. He spoke to essentially the same people about twenty years later than Amos, as described in the *Dictionary of Bible and Religion*:

> The Kingdom of Israel was deeply infused by the practices of Canaanite religion, which may even be mistaken for authentic Yahwism (belief in the Hebrew God) at local sanctuaries. Part of the practice of the fertility cult of Canaan was cult prostitution through which men and women alike sought to achieve union with God and to activate the growth of the crops through sexual union with the God Baal. When Hosea accused Israel of leaving God to play the harlot, he meant it literally.[3]

Amos's reaction to this situation was to tell the people they were sinning and God would punish them. He would then go into some detail on the nature of the punishment and suggest that they'd better stop before it got much worse. They were left with the image of a fuming, angry God.

Hosea begins his tale with a story. He married a woman, Gomer, and they had a covenant together – a commitment much like the marriage vows. But, Gomer broke the commitment by going into an adulterous relationship with someone else. Hosea believes she should be punished, but he loves her and does not want to cast her out of his life. He hopes and believes she will return to him and their covenant will be renewed, better than ever before.

Hosea, the teller of this story, is comparable in the story to God. Gomer, his adulterous wife, is Israel. Israel has left the entity that had given her life and hope. She went lusting after other gods, false gods (Baal), and religions of false promises. But rather than cast them into a fiery pit, God yearns for his people to return. God yearns to love them, teach them, and bless them:

I will heal their disloyalty;
I will love them freely,
for my anger has turned from them.

I will be like the dew to Israel;
he shall blossom like the lily,
he shall strike root like the forests of Lebanon.

His shoots shall spread out;
his beauty shall be like the olive tree,
and his fragrance like that of Lebanon.

They shall again live beneath my shadow,
they shall flourish as a garden;

they shall blossom like the vine,
their fragrance shall be like the wine of Lebanon. (Hosea 14:4–7)

James Luther Mays, who writes the introduction to Hosea in the *HarperCollins Study Bible*, concludes his essay with these words:

He proclaimed a searing and total punishment that would end the nation's career of promiscuity. But in an amazing way, Hosea saw behind the wrath of God a love that would not let the people be wiped out. The very judgment itself would take Israel back into the wilderness for a new beginning, a new covenant and a new gift of the land in a second history of reconciliation and regeneration.[4]

Reading the prophets is not easy, because their lives were based on assumptions we cannot even begin to imagine. But we can imagine that all of us will need as much forgiveness as we can find from anyone and from God. That understanding begins to grow in a few Biblical scriptures, and Hosea is one of them.

JEREMIAH

Jeremiah comes into the picture just before the Hebrew leaders are overwhelmed and carried off to Babylon. He was the son of a priestly family who came from a small village located not far north of Jerusalem. He believed devoutly that God had ordained his life from before his birth and had told him to warn the Hebrews of their coming defeat that will be brought about by their loose ways in lusting after other gods again. Jeremiah was a fairly gloomy guy who was also known as the "weeping prophet." In fact, the word "Jeremiad," which usually means a long, gloomy sermon about everything falling apart, comes directly from this Jeremiah.

I choose to include Jeremiah not because he is a prophet of gloom, but because of this passage:

> The word that came to Jeremiah from the Lord: "Come go down to the potter's house, and there I will let you hear my words." So I went down to the potter's house, and there he was working at his wheel. The vessel he was making of clay was spoiled in the potter's hand, and he reworked it into another vessel as seemed good to him.
>
> Then the word of the Lord came to me. "Can I not do with you, O Israel, just as this potter has done?" says the Lord, "Just like the clay in the potter's hand, so are you in my hand." (Jeremiah 18:1–6)

Traditional commentators suggest this passage is as dour as the rest of Jeremiah's teaching. People of Israel, if you think you have any independence or freedom in your judgments, think again. You are nothing more than clay in God's hands, and he can smash you to pieces if he is not pleased with you. More recently, interpretations of this passage have been much more helpful to contemporary men and women. We are continually shaped and molded as we grow older. We try out different versions of ourselves – just as a potter tries different versions of his work. If we don't like the direction in which we're going, we can call on God, Creativity, or our own intuition to help us mold in a different direction. Change – or redemption, as you will – is always possible.

In her book *Leadership in Turbulent Times*, Doris Kearns Goodwin studies the lives of four past presidents: Abraham Lincoln, Theodore Roosevelt, Franklin Roosevelt, and Lyndon Johnson.[5] She discovers that each man was born with significant ambition to be a leader. But early in adult life, each must learn to overcome serious setbacks that pose crises to his self-confidence. Their lives need to be reshaped – by God, Creativity, their internal fortitude, or some combination the three. As that reshaping process takes place, the qualities for which we now remember them become manifest. Jeremiah's metaphor was apt for his time and ours, though maybe it was not something Jeremiah had in mind at the time.

ISAIAH

Isaiah is the longest and arguably most influential prophetic book in the Bible. This is true partly because there are three authors of Isaiah. We know very little about any of them except that they lived somewhere between 742 and 701 BCE and contributed more to our common languages than any other book in the Bible. Here are some phrases from Isaiah that we recognize:

> For unto us a child is born
> Comfort ye, comfort ye my people
> Every valley shall be exalted
> The voice of him that crieth in the wilderness
> Surely he hath born our grief and carried our sorrows
> All we like sheep have gone astray

Isaiah had a great librettist; his name was Handel. The words reflect the Christian belief that significant parts of Isaiah express the conviction that Jesus was the Messiah anticipated by Isaiah. Needless to say, Jewish scholars and rabbis emphatically disagree. Here are some other phrases from Isaiah:

Swords into plowshares, spears into pruning hooks
Neither shall they learn war any more
The people that walked in darkness
The wolf also shall dwell with the lamb, and the leopard shall lie down with the kid . . . and a little child shall lead them.
They shall mount up with wings as eagles
Be of good courage
They shall see eye to eye
A lamb to the slaughter

There is one phrase that everyone associates with Isaiah that Isaiah didn't write. It is found as Isaiah 7:14: "Behold, a virgin shall conceive . . ." The word "virgin" was mistranslated. To early translators from the Hebrew, it meant "young woman." "Behold, a young woman shall conceive and bear a son." That woman may have been or may not have been a virgin. According to Davis, "Jewish commentators point out that Isaiah was specifically telling King Ahaz that his wife, the 'young woman' of the verse, would soon bear another son. That son was Hezekiah, who was a devout and good king, loyal to the traditions and obedient to the laws." Any *modern* translation of the Bible that is not published by a specific religion, including the *HarperCollins Study Bible* that is used by most seminaries and many colleges, agrees with this interpretation of Isaiah 7:14.

Now, Matthew interprets Mary as a virgin probably because he believes that Mary must have been a virgin to square what he wanted to believe about Jesus. Neither John, Mark, nor Paul seem to have believed in Jesus' virgin birth.

I raise this only because it raises the difficulty of translating the Bible primarily through the eyes of faith. Be that as it may, Isaiah – particularly the third Isaiah – gives us a hopeful vision of the future.

Finally, it is the conviction that despite our stupidity, foolishness, greed, and occasionally even evil inclinations, there is a chance for people who desperately want to change, to be made new. Amos lays out the ways in which people can fool themselves and violate the religious traditions upon which their nation is founded. Hosea assures us that God is prepared to hear our sincere regret and start over. Jeremiah dramatizes this with his metaphor of the potter and the clay. Isaiah imagines new and transforming leadership:

> The spirit of the Lord God is upon me,
>> because the Lord has anointed me;
> He has sent me to bring good news to the oppressed,
>> to bind up the brokenhearted,
> to proclaim liberty to the captives,
>> and release to the prisoners;
> to proclaim the year of the Lord's favor,
>> and the day of vengeance of our God;
>> to comfort all who mourn;
> to provide for those who mourn in Zion –
>> to give them a garland instead of ashes,
> the oil of gladness instead of mourning,
>> the mantle of praise instead of a faint spirit.
> They will be called oaks of righteousness
>> the planting of the Lord to display His glory.
> They shall build up the ancient ruins,
>> they shall raise up the former devastations;
> they shall repair the ruined cities,
>> the devastations of many generations. (Isaiah 61:1–4)

NOTES

1. Kenneth C. Davis, *Don't Know Much about the Bible: Everything You Need to Know about the Good Book but Never Learned* (New York: William Morrow, 1998), 221.

2. Martin Luther King, Jr. "I Have a Dream," speech, Washington, DC, August 28, 1963. Text of speech can be found in "American Rhetoric." http://www.americanrhetoric.com/speeches/mlkihaveadream.htm.

3. William H. Gentz, ed, *Dictionary of Bible and Religion* (Nashville: Abingdon Press, 1986), 467.

4. James Luther Mays, introduction to Hosea in *The HarperCollins Study Bible: New Revised Standard Version, with the Apocryphal/Deuterocanonical Books,* edited by Wayne A. Meeks et al. (New York: HarperCollins, 1993), 1331.

5. Doris Kearns Goodwin, *Leadership in Turbulent Times* (New York: Simon & Schuster, 2018).

CHAPTER 9

What Faith Really Means

The Psalms are the Bible's hymnal. Contrary to tradition, they are mostly not written by David but accumulated over the years, like the contributions to a denominational hymnal. In a similar fashion, they come in different styles and different moods, ranging from praise to angry lament. The Twenty-third Psalm is a song of praise and comfort, which is often used in hospitals, not infrequently at bedsides, and sometimes at funerals.

Albert Einstein once said that science can tell us a lot about the universe – how old it is, how vast it is, what laws of physics control it. But he went on to say that science is powerless to answer the most important question of all: Is the universe a friendly place, supportive of human hopes and aspirations?

Is the world a friendly place? We don't know for certain. I know, and I'll bet you know, people who believe that the universe is completely indifferent to whether we survive or not. Therefore, we must care for one another, for there is nothing else that will.

On the other hand, others believe that there is something – a spiritual force, a presence – in fact, we don't know what it is –

but there is something, and we depend on it. Our reliance on what cannot be seen, tested, or proved is called a faith. In the end, each of us — no matter what religion we belong to or regardless of whether we belong to any — is sustained by our faith in something unseen, unproven that allows us to get up and go about our business each morning.

By way of drawing out my point, I want to tell you a story of how I discovered some of my faith through the Twenty-third Psalm. When as a very young man, I served as a hospital chaplain. I bought myself a pocket Bible that I carried in my white coat. I had studied the Bible at divinity school but from a purely academic point of view. Personally and spiritually, I had no particular feeling for the book.

I wondered why anyone would want me to sit by their bedside and read aloud from the Bible, but chaplains carry Bibles and so did I. By the end of my internship, my pocket Bible opened automatically to the same page from which I was asked to read so many times beginning with, "The Lord is my shepherd, I shall not want."

It was the Twenty-third Psalm, one of the most popular psalms in the Biblical tradition. I confess, though, that for much of my ministry I disliked this psalm. The pastoral images of sheep and shepherd seemed distant and off-putting. As a backpacker, I had enough experience with green pastures to know that I did not want to lie down in one nor, for the same reason, did I want to be led beside the still waters. In fact, and this was the crux of my resistance, I did not want to be led at all. As a young man in his early twenties, I could not put my life experience within the psalm's embrace.

But somewhere along the way, in the second half of life, I think we become less the intrepid young adventurer and more the canny survivor. We learn that perils await us from which our education, good choices, common sense, income, professional status, and an army of friends, family, doctors, and mentors cannot protect us. When these perils strike, life does seem a dangerous place; we are suddenly grateful for any shepherd who helps us feel secure enough to retain our confidence in living.

What we look for in those tough moments is not someone to tell us what to do. We know we have to make our own decisions. What we look for – to use Rabbi Harold Kushner's words – is "a presence that makes the world seem less frightening."[1] By "presence," he means something that comes into our lives – a mood, an experience, or a place to which we go in our minds. It is an assurance we unmistakably feel though we cannot describe it. We do feel we are somehow being led.

"I shall not want." A modern translation of this phrase would be, "I have everything that I need." We want a lot of things in life. Wanting and working for something is part of the fun of living. I might want a trip to Europe, a complete set of *The New Interpreter's Bible*, a room to put it in, a house of my own on Cape Cod, and a lifetime of financial security. And that's just me getting warmed up. Each of us has lots of wants.

But the point of the passage is that I also have everything I need. There are relationships I cherish and work I enjoy doing. I am part of a life – and so are you – that is beautiful, intriguing, and challenging beyond all expectation. We have everything we need. To use Rabbi Kushner's words again:

> I shall often want. I shall yearn. I shall long. I shall aspire. I shall continue to miss the people and the abilities that are taken from my life as loved ones die and skills diminish. I shall probe the empty spaces of my life like a tongue probing a missing tooth. But I will never feel deprived or diminished if I don't get what I yearn for, because I know how blessed I am by what I have.[2]

"He makes me lie down in green pastures. He leads me beside the still waters." Another way of translating this passage

would be, "He allows me to lie down in green fields. He leads me beside the calm waters." As I did not entirely realize as a young man, these words were all entirely metaphorical.

You may have noticed that the habitable world is created in colors of green and blue. People who study such things tell us that these are very calming colors. On the other hand, we could not live in a world decorated completely in yellow, red, and purple. Being able to enjoy green pastures and calm blue waters – even to find them inspiring – is being able to live in the world on its own terms and to love it on its own terms. It is to be able to get up and look out, even on a midwinter's day at the start of the work week, and see something of beauty that is out there.

Having spent many summers on Cape Cod, I am impressed with how many people walk or drive down to the ocean at every season of the year just to gaze at the calm blue water. Every day the water looks pretty much the same as the day before. And yet looking into that depth of blue or in Vermont looking up into the green hues of the mountains acts on us like a tranquilizer. It is also a powerful reminder that something in the world is stronger and more purposeful than what we experience from our anxious lives. It restores our soul. So even though there are experiences in each person's life that can be alarming or even frightening, there is much in our world that calms and restores us and, when necessary, something leads us there.

The next phrase of the Twenty-third Psalm could be translated, *"He guides me on the paths of righteousness so that I may serve him with love."* It has been a contemporary conceit that there are no paths of righteousness – that all moral laws are culturally determined. According to this theory, we decide what's right and wrong according to what pleases us. But I think every healthy person knows that there are moral boundaries we must not cross. However it is that we know this, it is comforting to have a conscience that supports us against our own worst instincts – whatever they may be. It is frightening when our conscience deserts us. Therefore, we are grateful when we know that most often we are "guided" on the paths of righteousness by something that will not let us stray off the path.

"Though I walk through the darkest valley and stand in the shadow of death, I am not afraid, for I know you are always with me." Loss is inevitable, and death is inevitable. When we were younger and that shadow world rudely intruded into our happiness, we were devastated for a while; but then we managed to push it away and go on with our usually hearty denial of setbacks or death. That's perhaps as it should be. But in the second half of our lives, we become increasingly aware that the valley of the shadow is never far away. And of course, we are afraid to cross it. Most people are afraid to cross it.

I am remembering a woman from one of my congregations who had walked through that valley several times. She was also one of the most connected people in the congregation, giving strength to others and drawing it from them. Once a younger member asked her, "How do you do it? How does someone get through all of this sadness?" Her response was, "I don't know. You just do."

There could not have been a better response. "You just do" testifies to the strength that enables us to get up and walk day after day through the valley of the shadow until it is far behind us – at least for now. Different religious people make different choices about what to call their resources of strength. It could be God or inner strength or courage or pure cussedness, but my choice is that the words, "you just do" refer to what the psalmist meant by "thou art with me."

A modern translation of the next phrase is, *"You spread a full table before me even in times of great pain."* But for this phrase, I prefer the King James Version: "Thou preparest a table before me in the presence of mine enemies." Do we have enemies? Of course we do. All of us do. There are people who would like to rob us. There are people who would like to cheat us if they could. There are people who wouldn't mind hurting us. I'd call those enemies. There are also people who probably don't like us very much. Sometimes that disliking rises to a level that would suggest we probably should think of them as enemies, at least for the time being.

The knowledge that we have enemies presents us with some choices. We can give in to our enemies by becoming afraid or angry. We can become defensive toward everyone, thus further justifying the low opinion our enemies already have of us. Those are the easy choices. The hard choice is recognizing that life or God has laid such a table out before us that no enemy can diminish the value of what has already been given to us. Living fully and well is usually the best answer to having enemies.

I've not left out forgiveness as an option. The Christian scriptures, at least as Universalists read them, suggests that we forgive those who cherish unreasonable grievances against us just as God forgives everyone. I'm not there yet. We can try to forgive those who seem to cherish grievances against us, but we should also keep an eye on them.

If you are remembering the text, you'll notice that the psalmist has switched from speaking of God as an abstract principle and becomes much more personal. The presence of danger, enemies, and death has reminded him that this is a very personal relationship. One modern translation of these words would be, *"You feast me with your abundance and honor me like a king, anointing my head with sweet oil, filling my cup to the brim."*

A colleague of mine once remarked that because his father had called him "Champ" for all of the years of his growing up, the nickname stuck in his psyche as a description of what he could be. Though there were many times when the young man didn't as much as half believe he was a champ, there were tough times when that name – as a reflection of his parent's confidence – pulled him through. The psalmist is saying the same thing. Sometimes we feel that someone or something believes in us so much that we feel we will get through whatever difficulty lies ahead.

"Surely goodness and mercy shall follow me all of the days of my life, and I shall dwell in the house of the Lord forever." Richard Foster, who has written extensively about Quaker practices, remembers a time when he was a small boy, and his family was homeless. They had to spend a difficult winter in a mountain cabin that was heated only by a huge log fireplace.

Though it must have been a trying time for them, he remembers chiefly that every night he would fall comfortably asleep gazing into the blazing fireplace. He lay on the sofa under a heavy quilt and was profoundly grateful for the fire that was keeping the entire family warm and dry. He called these moments his "grateful center." The task of some of the psalms is to help us all find our own grateful centers. Or to put it in the words of fourteenth-century mystic Meister Eckhart, "If the only prayer you say in your whole life is 'thank you,' that would be enough."

So that's my faith best summarized in the Twenty-third Psalm. How did I get there? I fought against having any faith throughout my years as a young man and as a young minister. I steeped myself in academic theology trying to find the right one – the rational, intellectually defensible, systematic path to what I deeply believed. Eventually, I discovered that poetry, song, and life generally were leading me in the direction of my deepest, most heartfelt commitments. They were helping me discover the faith that has kept me going over so many years.

How do you know where your faith is founded? It is lodged in the words or music that will not let you go but come back to you over and over again. It is embedded in the silent prayers that get you through some of the most difficult times in your life. You cannot reason your way to it. It has nothing to do with whether or not you believe in God. It has to do with whatever gives you the strength to walk through that dark valley and emerge with the confidence to go on, even though you know there will be other dark valleys ahead.

If this were a workshop, I would give you a hymnal and ask if there is one hymn that you really love – even though you may not know why. And if the hymnal will not work for you, I would ask that you go through works of your favorite poet, or through pictures that are either photographed or drawn, or through memoirs of people reflecting on what has been important to them as they grow older.

Whatever will not let you go points toward the sources of the faith that has gotten you this far. May it grow, mature, and carry you along for the rest of your life.

NOTES

1. Harold Kushner, *The Lord is My Shepherd: Healing Wisdom of the Twenty-third Psalm* (New York: Random House, 2003), 27.

2. Kushner, 36.

CHAPTER 10

Life in the Thin Places

Every clergy person of any faith hears the complaint, "I prayed and prayed and prayed, and nothing happened that I prayed for." It's tempting to answer, "You prayed, yes, but did you listen? Were you somewhere where you could be quiet and listen?" The following reflection on Psalm 73 tells us that there are places for each of us where we can hear what we need to hear from the ultimate to which our prayers are addressed.

Modern translations of the Bible may not please everyone, but one modern rendition of Psalm 73 reflects that the people who wrote Psalms were like the rest of us. Their belief in the fairness of life and the fairness of God was often severely tested.

The psalmist, in modern idiom, began, "What's going on here? Is God out to lunch? Nobody's tending the store. The wicked get by with everything; they have it made, piling up riches. I've been stupid to play by the rules; what has it gotten me? A long run of bad luck, that's what – a slap in the face every time I walk out the door."[1]

The poet thought that any God worthy of the name would reward good people with respect and prosperity. The poet has lived that life of goodness and purity but with no significant increase in his prosperity or respect. And, it turns out that many people of whom the poet doesn't approve are healthier, wealthier, and more popular than he is. The passage continues, "I was looking up to the people at the top, envying the wicked who have it made, who have nothing to worry about, not a care in the whole wide world."

What kind of people are these folks, who seem not to have a care? They are "pretentious with arrogance; they wear the latest fashions in violence, pampered and overfed, decked out in bows of silliness. They jeer, using words to kill; they bully their way with words. They are full of hot air, loudmouths disturbing the peace." In other words, they give no thought to the physical, emotional, or political damage they cause. Yet, they seem to be very well off materially.

What's worse, because nothing attracts admiration then or now so much as financial success, "Therefore the people turn and praise them and find no fault in them." These arrogant folks believe their own press clippings. They have decided that what they can get away with has no limits.

It's not fair! If God is good and God is great, why doesn't God create a world where goodness prevails, badness is punished, and the weak are at least protected? The psalmist implies that he worried about this question for some time and finally realized that his ranting about the apparent injustices of the world was grating upon his friends and acquaintances. People were avoiding him.

"If I had given in and talked like this, I would have betrayed your dear children," he wrote. He would have depressed everyone within hearing distance. "Still, when I tried to figure it out, all I got was a splitting headache."

Many religious liberals come with this same set of concerns. Everyone knows that hypocrites and bullies exist, but some of us see and feel the injustice more deeply and desperately than everyone else. From childhood, we have been less able to shrug these things off. So, we become more skeptical about the goodness of God.

The playing field of life is not level. Some folks just don't have any good fortune, while others bend the rules and get more breaks than any human being deserves. Most people turn away from these injustices. They live comfortably without questioning the unfairness of what happens to others. They sing praises to a God who has been "good enough" to them. A few people like the psalmist tend to wander around questioning the kindness of God. They find no easy answers but are unwilling to give up their quest for justice.

How does the psalmist resolve his problem? He tells us, "I entered the sanctuary of God. Then I saw the whole picture." I know it seems like "I entered the sanctuary of God" is the standard religious answer, but let me suggest a different look at it. He is not referring to a specific "sanctuary" here. The psalmist is not saying, "Go to a house of worship, sign up, and make a pledge. Everything else will be just fine." The sanctuary of God is not a physical location. It is a *moment of time* in the psalmist's life when he can hear something more than his own voice. The sanctuary of God is a moment of time.

Something happens in that moment when he is so exhausted from entertaining his confusions and frustration that he finally gives up the fight to make sense. Having given up that fight, he feels that a Presence has come into his life. He feels spoken to though no words are ever used. We notice this because suddenly the language and tone of the psalm changes. The speaker is no longer talking about God in the abstract but is speaking in the first person to God. "I am still in your presence, but you've taken my hand. You wisely and tenderly lead me and then you bless me."

What happened in that moment of time that the speaker calls a sanctuary? What helped him to connect with a healing vision of his own life? This is what happened: he was so exhausted that he started to listen, and then he understood. As we know from human relationships, if we fill our thoughts with anger and recrimination or with demands that we be proven right, then we don't leave much room for anyone else to get in. We exclude family, friends, co-workers, and – very possibly – God.

Dr. Wallace W. Robbins, a Unitarian minister and former president of Meadville Theological School at the University of Chicago, once wrote:

> There are two reasons why God does not always answer prayer. The first is that so many people do all the talking that God cannot get a word in edgewise. The second is that too many people think they have the answer and spend their energy urging God to agree. God is not silent because God cannot speak, but because God is too polite to break up a filibuster or because God is dumbfounded to hear the extraordinary solutions which people urge upon the whole universe as a solution to their petty problems."[2]

My guess is that as long as we are instructing God on what we think we need and want to hear, God is silent. Our public prayers that seem to instruct God are actually for us, to remind us of our own spiritual condition. God does not need that reminder. The praise that we give in religious services is for our own benefit – reminding us that our spiritual and psychological health is vested in something much greater than our own anxieties and interests of the moment. God does not need the praise.

In the Biblical tradition, the doubts, anguish, and anger we sometimes direct at God has its own purpose. God can take the worst verbal abuse we can dish out, and we can dish it out for a lifetime if that is what we wish. However, we will sense the

Holy only when we are ready to finish laying out our case for help or justification.

Now we return to the question of what happened in the psalmist's sanctuary to enable him to receive a healing vision of his own life. We have learned that at various times the poet praised, prayed, ranted, raved, and screamed at God. Because he was not getting the kind of recognition he thought he deserved for being one of God's good guys, he decided the world was not working as it should work. Nothing came from all of this complaining. So, for a moment, he just gave up any notion that he alone would find the answer to his questions. It was that moment of utter defenselessness that made it possible for him to hear what had been spoken to him all along.

In the Celtic religious tradition, they believed that gods and humans live in two parallel worlds, but there are physical places where the two worlds almost intersect. These are called "thin spots in the universe" because for some reason when human beings go there, they are so awed that they do not fill up the air with protestations of their own worthiness. In these thin spots, people can put their petitions far enough away that they can be still, listen, and hear that the Holy has probably been speaking to them all along. You probably already know where the thin places in your own life are.

Harvard University's former preacher, the late Peter Gomes, has suggested that if we can imagine there are "thin places," physical places in the world where people feel more able to listen to the Sacred and be taught by it, then it seems likely there are situations in our lives that are like the thin places in the world. In those situations, we find ourselves more open to the kind of support that may come to us in unexpected ways.

Sometimes when we try too hard for something, we drive it away. For example, have you ever tried – and then strained – to remember a name or a fact that should come to you readily, but it won't come now? So you stop trying to find it in your memory bank. You even have to say to yourself, "I give up." Fairly shortly after that, the name or fact you wanted walks innocently through the door as if it were not aware it was ever missed.

The same principle applies to meditation or prayer. If you begin with the assumption that this "prayer thing" had better go to work and produce something you want, then you will be disappointed, because God is not a dot-com business. If you are willing to quiet that voice inside of you that really thinks it knows all the answers to your problems – to quiet that voice which is well defended against difficult questions – then you may find something in your thought you never expected to get from the silence.

Several times in my own life, I did find something. I had to admit to myself, "I'm out of solutions. I don't have a clue what I should do in this situation. Everything I try fails. I'm not even sure I have the right to keep trying." Having made that honest admission, something slowly crept into my thoughts that hadn't been there before. It wasn't a solution to my problem, but it was the courage to take next step.

At the time I wasn't trying to accomplish anything. I wasn't trying to reach God. I wasn't trying to solve a problem. In those moments when I admitted to myself that I completely could not find an answer I needed, then I entered into a calm that allowed a new approach to emerge along with a strange but good feeling that I was not alone.

Such an experience is counterintuitive for most of us. We want answers. We want to get stuff done. We want to know why the playing field isn't level for everyone and who is going to make it right. We want to know why bad things happen to good people and who is going to make that right. It may be that there are no neat answers to our questions.

It seems possible to me – it seems even likely – that all of creation has been given a radical freedom. Creation is wild and beautiful beyond the power of description. Creation endows all of life with incredible strength. Our longing for justice may be a reflection in us of God's love for creation. But bringing justice about is clearly our work to do. It does us no good to lament that the world is not perfect. An imperfect world was part of the original gift. How to live courageously in that imperfect world is wisdom we find only in the thin places in our life.

When the psalmist emerged from his sanctuary – from the thin places in his life where he was able to listen – he said he had learned three things. The first was that the people he had envied – those who lived on the surface of things and prospered – were truly "set in slippery places." Their happiness could not endure a time of difficulty, and times of personal difficulty are inevitable for all of us. The trappings of power and success do not, by themselves, shelter or sustain anyone.

The psalmist's second lesson was that the bitterness and envy he felt at seeing the good fortunes of others had rendered him – in his words – "stupid and ignorant" of the support that had been waiting in his life all along.

His third lesson was that the love he had looked for everywhere else would be constantly available to him in the thin places of life, where something speaks and we are finally able to listen. What is spoken may not be a solution, but it may be the next step along the way. And that's a lot.

I will close with this Celtic blessing:

> May you recognize in your lives the presence, power and light of your souls.

> May you (each) realize that you are never alone, that your soul in its brightness and belonging connects you intimately with the rhythm of the universe.

> May you have respect for your own individuality and difference.

May you realize that the shape of your soul is unique, that you have a special destiny here, that behind the facade of your life there is something beautiful, good and eternal happening.

May you learn to see yourself with the same delight, pride and expectation with which God sees you in every moment.[3]

NOTES

1. The modern translation of Psalm 76 throughout this chapter is from Eugene H. Peterson, *The Message: The New Testament, Psalms and Proverbs in Contemporary Language* (Carol Stream, IL: NavPress, 1995).

2. Wallace Robbins, *For Everything There is a Season: Meditations for the Christian Year* (Unitarian Universalist Christian Fellowship, 1978), 30.

3. John O'Donohue, "A Blessing of Solitude" in *Anam Cara: A Book of Celtic Wisdom* (New York: HarperCollins, 1997), 125.

CHAPTER 11

Filling in the Manger

We move now to the life and teachings of Jesus and begin with the nativity story. It is contained in only two gospels: Matthew and Luke. Their dramatic differences reflect their very different emphases as well as their intended audiences. For Matthew, Jesus was the Messiah who had been foretold by Jewish prophecy and was now at birth to be honored by visiting wise men. For Luke, Jesus was born in humble circumstances to poor parents and honored by those in humble circumstances. The different agendas of the four who wrote the gospels are a source of controversy throughout New Testament studies. However, in this sermon I will note that we have taken this story away from its authors and made it our own.

Many people who are curious about Unitarian Universalism ask, "Do you celebrate Christmas?" I always answer that we do. Most seem pleased with that answer. The next question they want to ask — I can see it trembling on their lips, but most often it goes unspoken — is, "But why?" If, as they were taught, Christmas celebrates the birth of Jesus Christ, who is considered by many to be the son of God and savior of us all; and if, as they have been told, we do not believe that about Jesus, how could we celebrate Christmas?

What we do believe about Jesus is that he seemed to have a profound sense of what we require to lead lives of integrity and compassion. He embodied his faith in the way he lived, and he died tragically, though setting an example by his life that would be nearly impossible for most of us to match – though we'd be a lot happier if we came even a little bit closer to his love of life and of his fellow human beings. We believe that when Jesus died, his disciples felt even closer to him. When they were gathered together, they sensed that he was there among them. But this was such a profound feeling that there was no way for them to express it except to tell stories of having seen him after his death.

We also believe that the celebration of Christmas is as much, if not more, about us and our relationships with one another. It is also more about our hopefulness and determination to lead better lives than it is about the details of Jesus' birth. So we celebrate, sing, and sometimes even live out parts of the Christmas story. It is a story of travelers, a story of seeking and establishing a home even where sometimes there is no welcome. It is about getting out of the cold. It is about a tale that, as far as anyone knows, is unique in the history of humankind.

Many Unitarian Universalist congregations celebrate Christmas quite vigorously and quite traditionally. When our present hymnal was published in 1993, some of the words to the carols had been rewritten to accommodate modern sensibilities. Many of us used the new hymnals that year, and the response among many UU congregations was overwhelming. They said, "We want the traditional carols." Even though our religious understandings may have changed, these carols link us to our own pasts and to generations before us who dared to believe that warmth and love could survive in this world. So let's look at the story and try to understand why it is so special and what it is telling us.

The stories in the gospels of Matthew and Luke are not history, of course. They are metaphorical. They represent, as clergyman and Christmas carol lyricist Phillips Brooks once put it so well, "the hopes and fears of all our years." The stories are about us. They are about the lonely voyage that each life is. We recognize this so well that we have put ourselves into these stories, and we call it Christmas.

Let us take a long look at the story that is reflected in the gospel texts and then see how we have fit ourselves into the larger story. Let's first approach the stable in Bethlehem, the one that has been depicted in paintings, poems, and songs and therefore has been etched into the back of our minds.

Snowdrifts and pine trees surround our stable. Our own hymn "In the Bleak Midwinter" depicts Joseph and Mary trudging through the bleak, frozen, midwinter landscape to find warmth and comfort in a snow-covered barn where they are sheltered from the wind by the trees of northern New England. I don't think it is just New Englanders who, from the richness of their imaginations, picture that stable as located actually somewhere near Woodstock, Vermont.

We know that Jesus was born in sunny Bethlehem, but most people prefer to site this story in the midst of the bleakness, the coldness, and the winter that actually surrounds their own lives. They supplement the bare framework of the story with an image of warmth coming to a shivering people, the warmth of a stable filled with love.

The storytellers recognize that we all are a shivering people. The bleakness outside the stable represents our inner weather, not Bethlehem's weather. We are hoping to come in out of the cold. Did you ever wonder why stables that are placed on church lawns at Christmas time are almost life-size? Many people want to imagine themselves inside the stable to live again the promise of a new life, a second chance, and the promise we make together to nurture that life.

Did you ever wonder, as well, what the big deal is about having a "white Christmas" – aside from the Bing Crosby song, that is? Could it be that the pristine whiteness of a newly fallen snow seems to promise a new start for all of us – just as the birth of a child seems to suggest that new births could happen in the rest of our lives? A new start is partly what Christmas means for many people.

According to the Biblical story, Jesus was *placed* in a manger. A manger was literally a feeding trough for animals. The story does not say that he was born in a manger, only that he was placed there.

The story does not say that he was *born* in a barn or in a stable. The manger could well have been located in a cave.

In our mind's eyes, however, we do not want to see the cold, damp walls of a cave. We want to see a stable that was built by human hands and hewn with an adze or a saw from rough wood, and we want to see it reflected in the light of torches. We want to give this child some greater shelter and warmth than the actual Jesus may have enjoyed.

We want to surround the manger with friendly animals. There are probably a hundred carols and short stories that have been written about the animals in the stable. However, the text does not say anything about animals being there. Perhaps this is because the people for whom the story was first written were not as sentimental as we are about animals. As far as they were concerned, the animals in a stable were just waiting to become food for the table. Our wanting to fill the stable with animals reflects our wish to see our own domestic pets as also creatures of God.

The story tells us that there was no place for Joseph and Mary in the inn. Thus, in every pageant, there is a child playing the innkeeper and saying, "No room." Then the innkeeper relents and brusquely offers Mary and Joseph a corner of his stable, because he believes the stable is a proper place for such lower-class trash, as they seem to be.

The innkeeper is a great sermonic device, but there is no actual innkeeper in the text. We created the innkeeper because we too often are the innkeepers of our own lives. We push new people and new experiences away. We fold our arms over our chests and say, "No room!" We need this story to remind ourselves who the innkeeper really is.

As we remember it and as we want to depict it on church greens and town commons, three kings from the east arrive in time to find the shepherds kneeling before the manger, awestruck at the birth of this child. Actually, this is a merger of two stories. Matthew tells us about the three kings who made the long journey, following a star to Bethlehem where they found that it shone over the *house* where Mary and Joseph lived. So the kings dropped in to Joseph's *house* to see the baby, have some eggnog, and leave some baby shower presents. But there was no inn, no crowds, no shepherds, and no manger in Matthew's story.

Luke tells us the story about the manger and the shepherds, but there are no magi in Luke's story. It seems clear that Matthew did not want shepherds in his story, and Luke did not want kings in his. But we have brought the stories together. We want both Joseph and Mary's journey and the magi's journey in the same story. We want high and low represented there.

Why do we want both of these journeys in the story we tell in our heads? For one thing, making a journey through the cold and darkness to a place of warmth and love is something many people traditionally do at this time of the year. At Christmas Eve services, we play host to a large number of travelers who will reach the end of their journey here at our inn.

More importantly though, we understand that life is a journey. Sometimes it is a dark and uncertain journey. We travel in search of a goal that is alternatively mysterious, elusive, and frightening. Along our journey there have been places filled with busy people going about their official business with no particular concern for us. There have been inns where we would have liked to stop and rest, but there was no room there for us. Our future travels contain the same possibilities and the same risks.

We travel with hope, and we bring gifts. We hope to be at ease with the shepherds and kings we may meet in life, and we hope that wherever our future resting places may be found, we will be not afraid when we get there. In other words, we craft elements of the Christmas story to speak to our own situations – our own longings for assurances that our journeys will be fruitful and that our lives will be illuminated by a faith we have found along the way. The very existence of this story in all of its warmth suggests that our faith is justified.

Let's just hear that story one more time, remembering that it is our story also. It begins with the song of Mary in which she expresses her pleasure that God should give the gift of creating life to a peasant woman. It is a rare moment, because in Mary's world most people believe that God does not traffic with the poor or with women. Already God is doing something to break up the old rules of might and power making right.

Then bureaucracy intervenes. The entire Roman world shall go to the places of their birth to be registered. This was the government's way of saying, "We want to keep tabs on you just in case we have not made your lives miserable enough." Mary and Joseph travel at the height of her pregnancy. Upon reaching their destination, they find there are more important people taking up the room in which they might have birthed their child.

So they find a crude alternative hiding place. This is fitting because, after all, as far as the town of Bethlehem is concerned, Jesus will be just another poor Galilean brat. This is a cynical world – not unlike our own – in which no one expects anything really hopeful to happen.

In the fields outside of town are shepherds who have no status at all because they take care of other creatures. It is to these people that an angel appears and speaks the words that characterize the soul of the Judaic and Christian traditions: "Be not afraid." Apparently, the angel believes that these peasants who actually care for other creatures are the only ones who can really receive and understand the message, "Be not afraid. You are not left alone."

Matthew tells us that Herod trembles when he hears that something about this newly born child is more important than he is. Therefore, the three kings are told in a dream that if they find the child, they must keep it to themselves. Matthew, who sees this story through the eyes of kings, knows that a power which does not belong to the king must be talked about very discretely, or the king will be angry.

On the other hand, Luke – who sees this story through the eyes of shepherds, people who have no orientation to or interest in power – instructs his shepherds to go out and tell the whole world. Luke believes that ultimately the Holy is stronger and more powerful than the apprehensions of dictators.

We don't know precisely where Luke and Matthew got their stories. They really aren't replicated anywhere else in the Hebrew tradition. But it is not difficult to see the inspirational source for what they wrote. That source is the central moral and spiritual message of the Jewish and Christian worlds. It is also what Unitarian Universalists inherit from that tradition.

Here is that message: Life is a precious gift. Along with this gift comes a mysterious strength. It is the strength of the Holy that dwells among us, and – if we are open to it – that strength enables us to use the gift of life well. Thanksgiving, care, compassion, and justice are its goals. Cynicism, manipulation, greed, and corruption will never be the last words. In fact, the next source of hopefulness or inspiration may very well be near to us. It may even come to us in the form of a person or an influence that will surprise us and challenge us before it comforts us.

Can we make that journey to Bethlehem again this year trusting in life's capacity to provide us with all that we really need? Can we find the openness expressed in the magi's presentation to a child? Can we find the faith expressed in the words from Luke's story, "Be not afraid"?

In the days to come, may you find the inn you seek, the company you cherish, the angels you need to hear, and the message that love is waiting for you somewhere. Do not be afraid.

CHAPTER 12

Your Wilderness Experience

We know very little about Jesus' early years. Joseph, his father, was probably more of a "handyman" than a carpenter, and Jesus undoubtedly followed him in his work. But Jesus also spent a good deal of time in the countryside and loved being there. Eventually, he realized that he was being driven to seek out the evangelist John and be baptized by him. It was at this point, when he was perhaps an older adolescent or a young man, that Jesus knew what his life was going to be. According to the story, it was here that he felt called by God.

The story that follows is not highly regarded by many because of its references to Satan. I am telling the story differently with my own spin, less concerned with satanic interpretations and more with the temptations most of us have to surmount in order to grow up.

Sooner or later, most of us will go on a wilderness journey. The journey I have in mind does not take us into the National Park System. I'm not suggesting the White Mountains. We won't need to bring along bug repellant, a flashlight, a sleeping bag, or a water filter. The only beasts we'll encounter will be those created by our own fears. These will be the beasts that populate everyone's wilderness: the internal beasts that puzzle or frighten nearly all of us.

Why would anyone take such a journey? Frankly, I'd rather stay home. But usually, we don't have much choice. It may be that a serious illness starts us on our way, or it may be the loss of a job. It may be the breakup of a marriage or a time of testing for our families.

It may be the betrayal of a false friend that hits us more seriously than most. It may be reaching that classic mid-point of our lives where we begin to look at our choices differently, and we look at our time left differently as it now seems to be running out. Perhaps none of this will happen to you, but my guess is that most people who have lived awhile will recognize in their own experience elements of what I am going to describe.

I started thinking along these lines many years ago when I attended a parents visiting day at Earlham College. I suspect it was to relieve the students from having to entertain their parents for forty-eight hours that the college offered classes on various subjects for the parents.

I attended a class on Dante's "Inferno," part of the epic poem about Dante's imaginary trip through Hell. As I looked around me, I realized most of us parents were about the same age. Then it hit me. In explaining the text and drawing us into conversation, he's talking about our own mid-life crises.

This fourteenth-century classic begins with the words, "In the midway of this our mortal life, I found me in a gloomy wood, astray, Gone from the path direct."[1] When Dante wrote "The Inferno," he was actually at the mid-point of his own life. The betrayal of false friends and former colleagues had caused him to question everything he had once believed.

He imagined that he was chased down into a vast hole by wild beasts that threatened to tear him limb from limb. He passes beyond a sign reading, "Abandon all hope, ye who enter here," and then he knows that he has reached the outer suburbs of Hell. This is his wilderness journey.

Descending into this hellish pit, he finds the trail winds downward like a canyon in the shape of a corkscrew. The upper, less severe circles of the canyon are populated largely by people whose prevailing sin has been only that they sometimes lost self-control. They acted hastily or without thinking – like most of us. And they have a chance to change their ultimate fate. In the lower circles are the folks who responded *too often* out of anger. They were known for their anger and were even proud of it. Lower still were those sins that were more calculated than passionate: the sins of cheats, thieves, seducers, and liars.

Lowest and worst of all were those whose sins involved carefully winning the deepest trust of other people and then betraying it. The temperature in Dante's Hell drops dramatically where it houses people with a diminished capacity for caring. At the lowest level are those who have killed in themselves all love for others. Their souls are encased in ice.

Like Dante, our own journeys begin with anger or rejection sometimes. They touch on deception, and they toy with indifference. We cycle through resentment and sadness because we are not happy to be in this wilderness. We are sure we shouldn't have to be in this place. Partly in response to those unpleasant feelings, we cycle through temptations to deceive other people or through even greater temptations to deceive ourselves.

It is at the final level – where indifference, disguise, or self-deception become so easy – that if we were lucky, we turned away and headed back slowly toward the light. Dante's classic descent into and escape from Hell has often been read as a Christian allegory. But it also can be read as a story of the psyche or the soul struggling to survive in a world that is both devious and beautiful, and in which we can be tempted by both. We have to learn how to give up the false security of deceiving others and ourselves in order to seem worthy of receiving their love.

Sometimes, our wilderness journey responds to challenges the world presents to us directly. This is what Jesus' wilderness journey was all about. It was, first of all, a metaphorical journey that many of us might recognize as a good description of the mid-life crisis. It came at a high point in Jesus' life just after John baptized him, and everyone said, "Surely this man is of God."

Then Mark tells us that the Spirit sent Jesus into the wilderness where Satan tempted him, and he was with the wild beasts – those wild beasts again – but the angels watched over him. That is all that Mark tells us, as though Mark believes that wild beasts and temptations happen to everyone, as I suspect they do.

Mathew and Luke tell us the fuller story. Reading between the lines, we suddenly know what is happening to Jesus that also happens to us in its own way. The first time Satan appeared to Jesus in the wilderness, he said, "If you are the Son of God, command this stone to become bread." The temptation was not to do a magic trick by turning stone into bread. The emphasis was on the word "if," as in, "*If* you are the Son of God, then *prove* it to us."

Sooner or later, we have to put away the idea that we need to prove ourselves to a crowd of real or imaginary observers. That is one of the great challenges of growing up. As young men and women, we often imagined that we were playing to a crowd of people who were relentlessly critical of our performance. Who knows if there was a crowd of observers or if they really were that critical? Once when I was a much younger minister, an older colleague said to me, "It may be of some comfort to you to know that the vast majority of your parishioners probably do not think of you at all during the week." That indeed was a comfort.

Nevertheless, believing that we do play to a crowd of critics, we want to please them. We want to say, "What will it take? What do I have to do to win your approval? When do I get to hear your applause?" It is the wrong question. The only real applause or assurance we can expect must come either from within ourselves or from God, who really already knows and loves us as we are. The first temptation that Jesus resisted was the temptation to allow himself to be defined by his need for approval.

Satan's next temptation was, "I will give you all of the power and the glory that you want *if* you will fall down and worship me." The imaginary audience does not applaud but instead keeps laying down new conditions that must be met before their approval will be gained. Just do this one more thing. Just climb a little higher on that ladder. The power and glory you receive will be our applause. Jesus declines this opportunity as well, because he knows that even the highest recognition that the world can give us – political, economic, or religious – will not offer us the ultimate assurances we want that our lives are important. Honors and recognition count for very little on the scale of what brings happiness. Real assurance and peace must come from within.

In the third temptation, Satan once again poses the great "if." "*If* you are who you say you are, jump down from this high place and float over the valleys below." Perhaps this is the temptation to believe that nothing really matters except one's own pleasure. If you can't win politically, if people won't appreciate you as much as you think they should, why not just live for yourself? Why not live only to make yourself happy?

This is the tough one. It is the point where we say, "Aw, the heck with it. You can't fight city hall because nobody cares. Why keep beating your head against the walls or trying to rouse troops that won't even save themselves?" This is the temptation that forces us to decide if we want to live by ends and goals that are beyond our self-interest. Do we want to live as a stream, flowing into and feeding other lives, or do we want to live only as a quaking bog?

Sooner or later, we all take a journey in which we test ourselves against what is unknown. If taking this journey sounds all very brave and daring, let me assure you that no one wants to go. No one really is ready for it. Moses ran away from his troubles and found an uncomplicated life caring for his father-in-law's sheep in a country far away from Egypt. Suddenly, a burning bush flared up beside him and told him to return to Egypt and take his people out of slavery. Moses didn't want to do that. He had found ways to be at least happy, and winning freedom for others wasn't high on his list of priorities. When God said to him, "Look, I'm giving you a chance to grow up," Moses responded, "Well, I don't know that I want to grow up. It's too hard." God said, in effect, "What made you think you had a choice? Go, and I will be with you."

Well, God may have sent Moses and his people into the wilderness, but the Spirit wasn't obviously there for them every time they wanted reassurance. When they were thirsty, they were directed to some water; but reaching the land flowing with milk and honey was withheld from them. When they were hungry, they were directed to some food; but it was not the great banquet they expected every time they turned around. When they sought reassurance and direction, they were told to elect leaders they trusted and then let them lead. That took some leap of faith. Most of our journeys will require a leap of faith as well – from what we know about ourselves and life to what we hope will be true.

While I was traveling through my own personal surgical wilderness in a bout with mouth cancer several years ago, I wish I could say that I found angels guiding me or voices reassuring me that everything was going to work out the way I wanted it to work out. That did not happen. Most of the time, what I did experience was a feeling that by taking one day at a time, I could handle whatever was coming and that whatever happened would be all right. So if I was led, it was not firmly by the hand but by gentle taps and pushes along the way. I don't know where those taps came from, but I trusted them.

Sometimes, we deliberately enter the wilderness to test our abilities to find our way out. Parker Palmer, a well-known Quaker educator, once wrote about taking an Outward Bound course to test himself. One day, he found himself leaning backwards out over a 110-foot cliff with a rope and harness over his body. In his own words:

> I was told to lean out over God's own emptiness and walk down the face of that cliff to the ground eleven stories below.

> I remember the cliff too well. It started with a five-foot drop to a small ledge, then a ten-foot drop to another ledge, then a third and final drop all the way down. I tried to negotiate the first drop; my feet instantly went out from under me, and I fell heavily to the first ledge. "I don't think you quite have it yet," the instructor observed astutely. "You are leaning too close to the rock face. You need to lean back farther so that your feet will grip the wall."

> That advice, like the advice of some spiritual traditions, went against my every instinct. Surely one should hug the wall, not lean out over the void! But on the second drop I tried to lean back; better, but not far enough, and I hit the second ledge with a thud not unlike the first. "You still don't have it," said the ever-observant instructor. "Try again."

> Since my next try would be the last one, her counsel was not especially comforting. But try I did, and much to my amazement I found myself moving down the rock wall. Step-

by-step, I made my way with growing confidence until, about halfway down, I suddenly realized that I was heading toward a very large hole in the rock, and − not knowing anything better to do — I froze. The instructor waited a small eternity for me to thaw out, and when she realized I was showing no signs of life she yelled up, "Is anything wrong, Parker?" as if she needed to ask. To this day I do not know the source of the childlike voice that came up from within me, but my response is a matter of public record: "I don't want to talk about it."

The instructor yelled back, "Then I think it's time you learned the Outward Bound motto." Wonderful, I thought. I am about to die, and she is feeding me bromides. But then she spoke words I have never forgotten, words so true they empowered me to negotiate the rest of the cliff without incident: "If you can't get out of it, get into it."[2]

Perhaps the wilderness journey nearly all of us must take is a test. The questions the test asks us to answer are: Can you trust yourself as you are? Can you trust the life you have been given and the resources you have been given to make life work for you and for others? Can you trust your ability to prevail over all that misleads, discourages, and sometimes defeats us? They're good questions for all of us to consider.

I've been lost in an actual wilderness several times − a wilderness with trees, bushes, rocks, mud, thickets, thorns, and no trail. I know that getting lost makes us feel stupid, scared, and sometimes close to panic. Then we must settle down to realize that we can't completely get out of it. We have to breathe deeply, think about next steps, get into it, and hope that we are led by gentle pushes and taps along the way.

NOTES

1. Dante Alighieri, *The Inferno*, translated by Rev. H. F. Cary (Benton Press, 2013), 3.

2. Parker J. Palmer, *The Active Life: A Spirituality of Work, Creativity, and Caring* (San Francisco: Harper & Row, 1990), 32-33.

CHAPTER 13

What Jesus Taught

Did Jesus even exist? There are those who believe Jesus may have been a myth created by a small group of people, and the myth grew in their hearts and minds to become the Christian savior. We can put this worry to rest. Nearly all historians accept that Jesus was real. There is evidence, provided by people who were not Christians, that Jesus lived, attracted a following, and was crucified. Some believed he survived the experience in spirit and appeared in body to his disciples.

Of far greater significance as evidence is the survival of the early Christian community at a time when it was competing with many other religions and being persecuted by some. Something happened to enable the earliest Christians to endure in the face of considerable doubt and opposition. We probably will never know what happened, and it will never meet our contemporary standards of proof. It was, however, not trivial. It changed lives. To dismiss it as trivial would be to misunderstand something that is still vitally important to many people.

What did Jesus believe, and where did those beliefs come from? Here is where we confront the issues of multiple authorships. The four authors of the gospels are identified as Matthew, Mark, Luke, and John. None of them knew Jesus. Mark may have been the closest in that he might have been a scribe to Peter during the last years of his life in Roman captivity. Mark's account is the earliest. We believe Matthew and Luke both had Mark's manuscript in front of them while they wrote their gospels, but they added material Mark had either not known about or chosen not to include. They all wrote within the first century of the Christian Era. John, whose gospel is completely different, wrote after the end of the first century.

But that's not the end of the authors. Over the years, other authors added their opinions, which makes reading the gospels rather unsettling because they contain points of view that seem not to be those of Jesus, the gospel writers, or of the age in which they wrote. They were written to encourage or threaten later Christians to stay faithful or be careful. While twenty-first century authors would not even think of mingling their thoughts without attribution in a document authored by someone else, this was not considered a problem for authors of the first, second, and third centuries who thought they were only improving an evolving work of Christian teaching.

What did Jesus actually say? What did he believe? This has also been the project of contemporary Biblical scholars, and they may never finish it. Reading their thoughts is a fascinating exercise if you have the time and patience.

In the early 1990s, a group of scholars went over the entire Christian testament, discussed each passage, then rated and color-coded each one as follows: red – that's Jesus, pink – sure sounds like Jesus, gray – well maybe, black – there's been some mistake. If this is something you want to read, then go for it. The book is *The Five Gospels: The Search for the Authentic Words of Jesus.*[1] Yet I think an easier way is by focusing on the work that many scholars believe is close enough to give us the full sense of what Jesus taught and how he might have been received.

Any author of a book with Biblical references must choose a translation of the Bible and announce it. Scholars argue considerably over translations, but I will not because I am not schooled in Aramaic, Hebrew, or Greek and because there are many other places to read these arguments. I think you didn't buy this book for that reason. I have chosen the translation *The Message: The New Testament, Psalms and Proverbs in Contemporary Language* by Eugene H. Peterson, a clergyman and a scholar whose work is generally well known. His book is sometimes received as a paraphrase of someone else's translation, but others point out that the author knew what he was doing and deliberately chose the modern idiom. He referred to it as a translation; in a front page of the book, he writes, "*The Message* is a contemporary rendering of the Bible from the original languages crafted to its present tone, rhythm, events, and ideas in everyday language."[2]

Most people understand that no one in Jesus' era spoke in Elizabethan English. Still, we've heard the King James Version of the Bible cited so often that when we hear that same passage translated into contemporary English, our first instinct is to figure that there is something radically wrong. If you would like to reassure yourself that we are talking about the same thing, feel free to consult any translation of Matthew: 5-7 and compare it with what follows.

We will be looking at what is commonly called the Sermon on the Mount. It appears early in Matthew's gospel and is, by most scholars' reckoning, actually a compilation of Jesus' teachings that are put together in this setting. Luke has a somewhat similar sermon, only it is written "on the plain" and can be found in Luke 6-7. Here is Peterson's translation of Matthew's version of the Sermon on the Mount:

> When Jesus saw his ministry drawing huge crowds, he climbed a hillside. Those who were apprenticed to him, the

committed, climbed with him. Arriving at a quiet place, he sat down and taught his climbing companions. This is what he said:

You're blessed when you are at the end of your rope. With less of you there is more of God and his rule.

You're blessed when you feel you've lost what is most dear to you. Only then can you be embraced by the One most dear to you.

You're blessed when you're content with just who you are — no more, no less. That's the moment you find yourself proud owner of everything that can't be bought.

You're blessed when you've worked up a good appetite for God. He's food and drink in the best meal you'll ever eat.

You're blessed when you care. At the moment of being care-full, you find yourselves cared for.

You're blessed when you get your inside world — your mind and heart — put right. Then you can see God in the outside world.

You're blessed when you can show people how to cooperate instead of compete or fight. That's when you discover who you really are, and your place in God's family.

You are blessed when your commitment to God provokes persecution. The persecution drives you even deeper into God's kingdom.

Not only that — count yourselves blessed every time people put you down or throw you out or speak lies about you to discredit me. What it means is that the truth is too close for comfort and they are uncomfortable. You can be glad when that happens — give a cheer even! — for though they don't like it, I do! And all heaven applauds. And know that you are in good company. My prophets and witnesses have always gotten into this kind of trouble.

There are two major concerns here. The first is that our preoccupation with our self and our pride of status or accomplishment is what stands between us and any sense of the transcendent.

The second concern is for Jesus' core of disciples, who apparently have been subjected to ridicule and other forms of abuse because they followed him. He wants them to understand that they are doing the right thing and God does care about them. The passage in Matthew continues:

> Let me tell you why you are here. You are here to be the salt seasoning that brings out the God-flavors of this earth. If you lost your saltiness, how will people taste Godliness? You've lost your usefulness and will end up in the garbage.

> Here's another way to put it: You're here to be light, bringing out the God colors in the world. God is not a secret to be kept. We're going public with this, as public as a city on a hill. If I make you light bearers, you don't think I'm going to hide you under a bucket, do you? I'm putting you on a light stand. Now that I've put you there on a hilltop, on a light stand – shine! Keep open house; be generous with your lives. By opening up to others, you'll prompt people to open up with God, this generous father in heaven.

Jesus then speaks to the concern that he has come to defy God's law. He has actually come to complete God's law. Matthew is a Jew who is writing for Jews who might be convinced that Jesus is their prophet if not their Messiah. This point is very important to him.

Jesus also points out that the commandment not to murder should not be interpreted legalistically. Anyone who nurses angry thoughts is guilty of "murder" as much as anyone who takes the life of another. He then says:

> Or say you are out on the street and an old enemy accosts you. Don't lose a minute. Make the first move; make things right with him. After all, if you make the first move to him, knowing his track record, you are likely to end up in court, maybe even in jail.

Jesus also believes in marriage, and he believes in those who merely observe the legal niceties of marriage until they take advantage of existing laws regarding divorce, which were fairly permissive at this time. He says:

> Remember the scripture that says, "Whoever divorces his wife, let him do it legally, giving her divorce papers and her legal rights"? Too many of you are using that as a cover for selfishness and whim, pretending to be righteous just because you are legal. Please no more pretending. . . . You can't use legal cover to mask a moral failure.

The passage in Matthew continues:

> And don't say anything you don't mean. This counsel is embedded deep in our traditions. You can only make things worse when you lay down a smoke screen of pious talk, saying, "I'll pray for you," and never doing it or saying, "God be with you" and not meaning it. You don't make your words true by embellishing them with religious lace. In making your speech sound more religious, it becomes less true. Just say "yes" and "no." When you manipulate words to get your own way, you go wrong.

Jesus is suggesting that the way we use words changes the way we feel about what the reality of the situation really is and may place a barrier between ourselves and others. Therefore, saying "I'll pray for you" and not really meaning it diminishes the honesty of our relationships. I have noticed that every contemporary reform movement – anti-racism for example – creates its own language that exalts some and diminishes others, creating needless separations. Matthew 6 continues:

> Here's another old saying that deserves a second look: "eye for an eye, tooth for a tooth." Is that going to get us anywhere? Here's what I propose. Don't hit back at all. If someone strikes you, stand there and take it. If someone drags you into court and sues for the shirt off your back, gift wrap your best coat and make a present of it. And if someone takes unfair advantage of you, use the occasion to practice the servant life. No more tit-for-tat stuff. Live generously.

This may be the hardest teaching for us to accept. As children we – boys and increasingly girls – were taught to defend ourselves. I've noticed that many of the children in the congregations I served are being taught martial arts, partly because it's good physical discipline and largely because of school bullies. So what do we do? Perhaps the passage gives us something to think about and perhaps to differentiate between those who oppose us but could be handled and even befriended in a gentler way and those whose appreciative attention can only be gotten initially, at least, through force.

> You're familiar with the old unwritten law "love your friend" and its unwritten companion "hate your enemy." I'm challenging that. I'm telling you to love your enemies. Let them bring out the best in you, not the worst. When someone gives you a hard time, respond with the energies of prayer, for then you are working out of your best selves, your God-created selves. This is what God does. He gives his best – the sun to warm and the rain to nourish – to everyone regardless: the good and the bad, the nice and nasty. If all you do is love the loveable, do you expect a bonus? Anybody can do that. If you simply say hello to those who greet you, do you expect a medal? Any run-of-the-mill sinner does that.

In a word, what I'm saying is, "Grow up." You are kingdom subjects. Now live like it. Live out your God-created identity. Live generously and graciously toward others, the way God lives toward you.

In case it hasn't jumped out at you yet, the phrase "live generously and graciously toward others, the way God lives toward you" illuminates much of Jesus' teaching. What does it mean to live generously? What does it mean to live the opposite way – say miserly? What is it like to be generous to others apart from what we may offer them in the worth of goods and services? And what is it like to be stingy in any way? Most importantly, what does it do to our soul or psyche when we are generous or when we are not generous? The passage continues:

> Be especially careful when you are trying to do good so that you don't make a performance out of it. It might be good theater but the God who made you won't be applauding.

> When you do something for someone else, don't call attention to yourself. You've seen them in action I'm sure – play actors I call them – treating prayer meeting and street corner alike as a stage, acting compassionate as long as someone is watching, playing to the crowds. They get applause, true, but that's all they get. When you help someone out, don't think about how it looks. Just do it quietly and unobtrusively. That is the way your God who conceived you in love, working behind the scenes, helps you out.

> And when you come before God, don't turn that into a theatrical production either. All these people making a regular show out of their prayers, hoping for stardom! Do you think God sits in a box seat?

Once again, Jesus is reminding us to be spiritually honest. It is not the words we say in prayer or sing in hymns, but the feeling that we mean it. This is the difference between hypocrisy and the truth of our spiritual lives. For Jesus, by being true to our spiritual self, we will eventually come closer to God. Indulging in hypocrisy, we drift farther away from that core and from our best selves. The passage continues:

> Here's what I want you to do: find a quiet secluded place so you won't be tempted to role-play before God. Just be there as simply and honestly as you can manage. The focus will shift from you to God, and you will begin to sense his grace.

> The world is full of so-called prayer warriors who are prayer ignorant. They are full of formulas and programs and advice, peddling techniques for getting what you want from God. Don't fall for that nonsense. This is your father you are dealing with, and he knows better than you what you need. With a God like this loving you, you can pray very simply like this:

> Our Father in heaven,
> Reveal who you are.
> Set the world right;
> Do what's best ---
> As above, so below.
> Keep us alive with three square meals.
> Keep us forgiven with you and forgiving others.
> Keep us safe from the Devil and ourselves.
> You're in charge!
> You can do anything you want!
> You're ablaze in beauty!
> Yes. Yes. Yes.

> In prayer there is a connection between what God does and what you do. You can't get forgiveness from God, for

instance, without also forgiving others. If you refuse to do your part, you cut yourself off from God's part.

When you practice some appetite denying discipline to better concentrate on God, don't make a production out of it. It might turn you into a small-time celebrity, but it won't make you a saint. If you go into training inwardly, act normally outward. Shampoo and comb your hair, brush your teeth, wash your face. God doesn't require attention-getting devices. He won't overlook what you are doing; he'll reward you well.

Don't hoard treasure down here where it gets eaten by moths and corroded by rust – or worse! – stolen by burglars. Stockpile treasure in heaven, where it is safe from moth and rust and burglars. The place where your treasure is, is the place you will most want to be, and end up being.

Your eyes are windows into your body. If you open your eyes wide in wonder and belief, your body fills up with light. If you live squinty-eyed in greed and distrust, your body is a dank cellar. If you pull the blinds on your windows, what a dark life you will have!

You can't worship two gods at once. Loving one god, you will end up hating the other. Adoration of one feeds contempt for the other. You can't worship God and money both.

If you decide for God, living a life of God-worship, it follows that you don't fuss about what's on the table at mealtimes or whether the clothes in your closet are in fashion. There is far more to your life than the food you put in your stomach, more to your outer appearance than the clothes you hang on your body. Look at the birds, free and unfettered, not tied down to a job description, careless in the care of God. And you count far more to him than birds.

Has anyone by fussing in front of the mirror ever gotten taller by so much as an inch? All this time and money wasted on fashion – do you think it makes that much difference? Instead of looking at the fashions, walk out into the fields and look at the wild flowers. They never primp or shop, but have you ever seen color or design quite like it? The ten best-dressed men and women in the country look shabby along side them.

If God gives such attention to the appearance of wildflowers – most of which are never seen – don't you think he'll attend to you, take pride in you, and do his best for you? What I am trying to do here is to get you to relax, to not be so preoccupied with the experience of getting, so that you can respond to God's giving. People who don't know God and the way he works fuss over these things, but you know both God and how he works. Steep your life in God-reality, God-initiative, God-provisions. Don't worry about missing out. You'll find that your everyday human concerns will be met.

Give your entire attention to what God is doing right now, and don't get worked up over what may or may not happen tomorrow. God will help you deal with whatever hard things come up when the time comes.

This is the end of chapter 6 in Matthew. If the scribes who were piecing together this literary masterpiece were writing an actual sermon, the way preachers have to every week, this would be the ending. From my perspective, here is the clearest, down-to-earth expression of Jesus' message: Don't worry. Just look – open your eyes and look. See the world that God has laid out for you and understand that in the larger scale of things, God will take care of you.

Of course, there is another chapter to the Sermon on the Mount that can be found in any number of translations in any library or bookstore. Here is my summary: God has bestowed God's love on all of creation including each of us, those closest to us, our neighbors, our friends, and our enemies. Our response to God's love must be to respond to others with heightened respect, care, and concern.

Since none of us is perfect, our readiness to forgive is an important part of who we are if we hope to be forgiven. This means we must live generously toward ourselves and toward others, remembering that the magnitude of what we are given in this life is vastly more important than what we think we want.

And finally, we must be honest with ourselves, our companions, and with what we ask of God in prayer. Jesus goes on at some length about the hypocrisy he sees around him. If we create a front of virtue or piety before others, how can we be honest with God?

NOTES

1. Robert W. Funk, Roy Q. Hoover, and the Jesus Seminar, *The Five Gospels: The Search for the Authentic Words of Jesus* (New York: MacMillan, 1993).

2. Eugene H. Peterson, *The Message: The New Testament, Psalms and Proverbs in Contemporary Language* (Carol Stream, IL: NavPress, 1995).

CHAPTER 14

The Sacrament of Parables

Jesus often spoke in parables. A parable is a story that you have to live with for a while before its meaning suddenly becomes clear. This frustrated his disciples at first, and they probably asked, "Why don't you just say what you mean?" Perhaps Jesus understood that there are many things we don't really know until we can work them out for ourselves. This chapter will present a small selection of Jesus' parables.

Many years ago, a colleague of mine wrote a paper on the sacrament of preaching. He was essentially holding up the experience many preachers have had in which a parishioner remembers with appreciation a sermon we gave and tells us specifically what he got from it. What's puzzling is that we know we never said that. We know it wasn't even in our minds to say that. So from where did the thought come?

Somewhere in between the minister's desire to communicate and the parishioner's desire to receive, the experience gives a message. Often, it turns out to be vitally important. It is a message neither of them expected. A "sacrament" occurs when a feeling or thought that seems terribly important and comes out of a very ordinary experience is suddenly filled with meaning. Many of us would say that something of the Holy is involved in this experience.

There were many reasons why Jesus told stories, but this sacramental nature of parables is the most important one. It is also true that most people love to hear stories. It's a lot easier to listen to and contemplate the parable of "The Good Samaritan" than it is to hear a preacher announce, "You must help people in trouble." In fact, stories equalize the social distance between the storyteller and the listener. In the stories that Jesus told, there is often a dramatic turn of events between what the storyteller leads you to expect and where the story ends. In the end, the tables are turned. The listener must ask and try to answer, "Why?"

Most of Jesus' parables do not employ religious images or concepts. Many of the people who listened to him were not looking for conventional religious reassurance. Had they heard such bromides from him, they would not have followed him. And while it is true that some of Jesus' parables do have conventional religious endings – for example, "This is what I mean by the 'Kingdom of God'" – many scholars believe they were added by later writers who were concerned that Jesus left the meaning of his parables to individual listeners.

THE PARABLE OF THE SOWER

A congregation I once served as an interim minister worshipped in a beautiful late nineteenth-century building. High over the pulpit and altar was a stained glass window picturing a farmer scattering seeds. I asked several members of the congregation what they thought the window was intended to symbolize, but no one I spoke to seemed to have thought much about it. Here is the parable that it represents:

He began to teach them many things in parables, and in his teaching he said to them: "Listen! A sower went out to sow. As he sowed, some seed fell on the path, and the birds came and ate it up. Other seed fell on rocky ground where it did not have much soil, and it sprang up quickly, since it had no depth of soil. And when the sun rose, it was scorched; and since it had no root, it withered away. Other seed fell among thorns, and the thorns grew up and choked it, and it yielded no grain. Other seed fell into good soil and brought forth grain, growing up and increasing and yielding thirty and sixty and a hundredfold."

And he said, "Let anyone with ears to hear listen!" (Mark 4:1-9)

Any parable can lend itself to several interpretations. As a preacher, I always suspected that the stained glass window of the sower in the church where I served was intended to suggest that the parishioners – who in the nineteenth century would have been more familiar with the parable than many are today – would have given some thought to what he/she brought along to the worship experience. Some come to worship with spiritual soil that has been hardened by the passage of many people and events passing over it. It has been hardened also by ideas that no longer work for the worshippers, but they cannot seem to let them go.

Some come to worship with rocky ground in their spiritual soil. They jump into our arms proclaiming that they have finally found what they have been looking for, but then they disappear and reappear thereafter only occasionally. Eventually, they leave altogether. Their newfound faith did not find enough spiritual soil in which to grow and ripen.

Others come to worship with thorns in their soil. Perhaps resentments or misunderstandings from their childhood or from their everyday lives or perhaps resentments toward their congregation or minister make it difficult for them to accept an allegiance to what seems more promising.

Finally, there are seeds that fall on good soil – soil that has been carefully prepared by thought, perhaps by prayer, and possibly by openness to the possibility that something new won't hurt.

However, there are other possibilities. Perhaps the parable was also directed to those disciples who were trying to recruit converts to his cause and were becoming discouraged because of the indifference or mockery that they often met. His advice to them would readily be recognized by people who have spent a significant part of their lives trying to lift up a cause that seems vitally important to them but has not yet caught fire among their peers.

Marcus Borg, in his book *Conversations with Scripture: The Gospel of Mark*, suggests how the beleaguered supporters of some unpopular causes would have received this parable:

> The parable could explain why only a relative few have responded to the message of the kingdom. Only some hearts are fertile.
>
> The parable could provide encouragement to keep on sowing the seed of the kingdom. Although some seed will land on infertile ground, some will thrive and multiply. You never know which is which.
>
> The parable could offer counsel in the face of discouragement. This is like the interpretation above with an additional nuance: don't be discouraged. Keep on keeping on.
>
> The parable raises in the minds of the hearers: What kind of ground or soil are we? Do we hear and respond to the word of the kingdom differently because of the kind soil we are? And is it possible to become a different kind of soil?[1]

There is a third possible approach that focuses on the sower rather than the listener. It is that this sower of seeds is so radically giving, so affirming, that seed are scattered everywhere without judgment concerning where it might best settle and be nurtured. Where you go with this or any other parable is up to you.

One thing is clear. Jesus understood probably a lot more about his natural environs than other spiritual leaders of his day, and that certainly enriches our understanding of what he taught.

LOST

I joined the Boy Scouts when I was eleven, and one of the first things I did was sign up for a hike on the Appalachian Trail in northeastern Pennsylvania. I was probably one of the youngest boys on the hike and was having difficulty keeping up with the others. I was struggling on an uphill. At some point, the scoutmaster picked up the pace, and they all walked up the trail away from me until everyone was out of sight.

To be left in that situation without anyone looking back is humiliating. The message clearly was, "We don't know why you're on this hike, but we'd just as soon leave you behind than have to wait for you." Fortunately, I had been on enough trail hikes to know that I should follow the blazes. Even so, if I had come to an intersection or an ambiguous part of the trail, which happens on trails, I wouldn't have known which way they went. If I had fallen and twisted my ankle or come too close to a rattlesnake, which also happens in these woods, I would have had no one around to know or care.

All of these thoughts crowded through my mind and made for at least an hour of very unpleasant walking. At any moment I expected to see that someone had come back to see how I was doing and if I was all right. But that did not happen. Eventually, I found them waiting by the trail somewhat impatiently – as they made clear to me. At the end of the trip, I left the scouts for good. For many of my adult years, I led Appalachian Trail trips for a summer camp. I always made sure that I was the last person in line, no one got behind me, and the camper in front of me had a very pleasant conversation with someone who cared about how the trip was going for him.

Jesus was very concerned about relieving the pain and alienation of becoming lost, and he told several parables about it, including the parable of the prodigal son. But first, let's look at the parable of the lost sheep.

THE LOST SHEEP

Now all the tax collectors and sinners were coming to listen to Jesus. The Pharisees and scribes were grumbling and saying, "This fellow welcomes sinners and eats with them." So, Jesus told them this parable:

> Which one of you having a hundred sheep and losing one of them, does not leave the ninety-nine in the wilderness and go after the one that is lost until he finds it? When he has found it, he lays it on his shoulders and rejoices. And when he comes home he calls together his friends and neighbors, saying to them, "Rejoice with me, for I have found my sheep that was lost." Just so I tell you, there will be more joy in heaven over one sinner who repents than over ninety-nine righteous persons who need no repentance. (Luke 15:1-7)

The story is an allegory, of course. Jesus' listeners would have assumed that a man with one hundred sheep must be a very rich man and could well afford to lose one of them. Searching the woods and fields alone for that missing sheep held its elements of risk, which he could well afford to avoid by just writing off that lamb. But the man does not do this. Every member of his herd is important to him, and he will not be happy until he has found the lost sheep. And we, by implication, should know that those with whom we share this journey of life are not disposable. No matter how difficult, confusing, or off-putting we may find them to be, we need them, and they need us. No one, as we shall see in the prodigal son parable, can be written off.

This story is often read as a parable about who will get into the kingdom of God. We may never know if this was Jesus' real intent or if Luke or someone "improving" upon the Gospel of Luke attributed that intent to him. I believe that for Jesus, the kingdom of God was a state of mind; they who genuinely wanted to enter in would feel welcomed if they did.

THE MAN WHO GAVE A PARTY

According to Luke, Jesus and his disciples were talking about who would be entitled to enter the kingdom of God. In fact, the disciples were somewhat obsessed by this thought. Then Jesus said:

> . . . someone gave a great dinner and invited many. At the time for the dinner he sent his slave to say to those who had been invited, "Come, for everything is ready now." But they all alike began to make excuses.
>
> The first said to him, "I have bought a piece of land, and I must go out and see it; please accept my regrets."
>
> Another said, "I have bought five yoke of oxen, and I am going to try them out; please accept my regrets."
>
> Another said, "I have just been married, and therefore I cannot come."
>
> So the slave returned and reported this to his master. Then the owner of the house became angry and said to his slave, "Go out at once into the streets and lanes of the town and bring in the poor, the crippled, the blind and the lame."

> And the slave said, "Sir what you have ordered has been done, and there is still room."
>
> The owner replied, "Go out into the roads and lanes and compel people to come in, so that my house may be filled." (Luke 14:15-23)

The beginning of this story replicates the worry of many fairly well-off people who plan a party and want to invite other well-off people they like, people they would like to get to know better, and people they want to impress. But all the prospective guests have excuses. Commentators differ on whether these are legitimate excuses or fabricated to get them out of the obligation to attend this host's party.

One man has bought five yoke of oxen he says he has never seen before. That seems naïve, as is the man who has bought land he has not seen. Besides, the land is not going anywhere. It will be there tomorrow. The man who's just been married gets a pass on this one. But the typical host would be hurt and offended; his first thought would be to find a way to exact vengeance on his ungrateful friends.

Instead, the man asks the slave to go at once and bring in the "poor, the crippled, the blind and the lame." When told later there is still room, he asks his servant to go out and bring more folk in who would enjoy being guests, which they hardly ever expect to happen. Now this story is told at a banquet where Jesus must have noticed that his disciples probably pushed each other out of the way in order to occupy the places of honor at the table themselves.

Jesus' response was to remind them – through this parable – that all are welcome at the table. For those who have much, this may not seem terribly important; but those who have little will understand and appreciate what they have been given.

In her book *A Woman Reads the Gospel of Luke*, Loretta Dornisch makes the following comment on this passage:

The banquet . . . images are pointing to the kingdom both present and to come. It is a banquet and a kingdom for everyone where justice will prevail. Women will not be excluded, nor will those who are poor, maimed or blind. It is something unheard of to have such a societal reversal! The world is turning upside down.[2]

THE GOOD SAMARITAN

The Good Samaritan is one parable that nearly everyone knows. In some localities there are even "Good Samaritan laws" to protect people from prosecution who might have rendered assistance to someone else who later may not be grateful for the care he got. From Luke:

> Just then a lawyer stood up to test Jesus. "Teacher," he said, "what must I do to inherit eternal life?" He said to him, "What is written in the law? What do you read there?" He answered, "You shall love the Lord your God with all your heart and with all your soul, and with all your strength, and with all your mind; and your neighbor as yourself," And he said to him, "You have given the right answer; do this and you will live."
>
> But wanting to justify himself, he asked Jesus, "And who is my neighbor?" Jesus replied, "A man was going down from Jerusalem to Jericho, and fell into the hands of robbers, who stripped him, beat him and went away, leaving him half dead. Now by chance a priest was going down that road; and when he saw him he passed by on the other side. So likewise, a Levite, when he came to the place and saw him, passed by on the other side. But the Samaritan, while traveling came near him; and when he saw him, he was moved with pity. He went to him and bandaged his wounds, having poured oil and wine on them. Then he put him on his own animal, brought him to an inn and took care of him. The next day he took out two denarii, gave them to the innkeeper, and said, "Take care of

him and when I come back I will repay you whatever more you spend." Which of these three, do you think, was a neighbor to the man who fell into the hands of the robbers?" He said, "The one who showed him mercy." Jesus said to him, "Go and do likewise." (Luke 10:25-37)

According to Amy-Jill Levine in her book *Short Stories by Jesus*, "The road from Jerusalem to Jericho was an eighteen-mile rocky path that descended from 2500 feet above sea level to Jericho's 825 feet below. . . . Even those who had never traveled the road . . . knew about its dangers and its possibilities."[3]

Those who passed by "on the other side of the road," the priest and the Levite, were not prevented by their religious beliefs or practices regarding the dying or dead from stopping to help the stricken traveler. Perhaps they were in a hurry to meet other commitments. Who knows? They simply chose not to stop, as we too sometimes have chosen not to stop after briefly weighing the problems we might encounter by stopping to help someone. And then we moved on.

Finally, and most importantly, the Samaritan was not just another minority. Samaritans were a despised minority, a hated minority. So for Jesus to tell a story in which the only person to do the decent thing for a beaten traveler was from a minority of which they expected nothing either good or decent, this would have been very hard for them to accept. Yet sooner or later, we all have to accept that those about whom we nurse angry beliefs may actually be quite different from our presuppositions. And he/she may be our neighbor.

Through his parables and talks, Jesus challenges some of the cherished assumptions of those who follow him. How does he get away with this, as honored and loved as we know he was by his friends and disciples? I believe he incorporated everything he taught into who he was with those who came to know him.

They probably couldn't understand it or explain it, but he was in himself everything he asked them to be.

THE PRODIGAL SON

I will tell this story in my own words, but you're welcome to look it up in Luke 15:11-32.

Once there was a man who had two sons. One day the younger son came to him and said, in effect, "Father I'm not getting any younger, and you're not dead yet. Why don't you give me my share of the inheritance now, so that I can go off and make my fortune in the world?" Well okay, I've changed his words a bit, as I will do in other parts of the story, but the gist is very much here. Despite the insulting manner in which this request is made, the father complies and gives his son the money.

The younger son goes off and thoroughly wastes his father's money in riotous living. Going to live in a foreign land, he acquires a large number of friends and imagines himself a most popular fellow until his money runs out. And when he had spent all of his inheritance, it turned out that a famine swept the land, and he was both penniless and starving. The only job he can find is caring for hogs, which for a young Jewish man suggests the worse of outcomes. So the young son decides to go back to his father. The story tells us how he rehearses what may have been an insincere apology that he will make to get into his father's good graces.

It appears that the father has spent a lot of time waiting and looking for him, for as soon as the prodigal son appears over the horizon – and before he even has the chance to make his contrition speech – the father rushes to embrace him. He then orders up a huge banquet and invites all of the neighbors to join in.

Now the older son who has been working dutifully at his father's side for many years apparently did not hear about the party. He is trudging back from the fields when he sees there is a party going on. A huge tent has been erected. There are chairs and tables laden with food under it, and a rock band is playing. The party is in his wastrel brother's honor.

The older son reproaches his father. He says, "Father, I have been here at your side – the paragon of faithfulness – for lo these many years, but my younger brother arrives and you kill the fatted calf and have a party." And the father says to him, "Son, you are always with me, and all that is mine is yours. It is fitting to make merry, for your brother was dead and now is alive."

This is a story that gets to most of us in one way or another. Many of us have siblings and may have had moments when we felt that our siblings received most of the good things in the family relationship. At first glance, many would agree that the father's solution – to reward the undeserving and at best ignore the deserving – may not be good parenting in that it does not accord with our sense of justice.

We can tell from reading the gospels that the disciples were also very concerned with justice. It appears that they argued over every little thing. But it is significant that the father in this story does not wait to hear his son's arguments for wasting his inheritance and nearly ruining his life. He is not interested in adjudicating the fairness of what he is about to do. Perhaps he knows there is no ultimate fairness. Perhaps there is only love and death.

The father is determined to live out his love for his sons regardless of what happens. Like the man who gave a party that no one attended, he is living generously no matter how much provocation he may have been given to do otherwise. Like the Samaritan, he will serve life over death at any cost.

Whatever else we know or think we know about Jesus, we know he followed this particular path – celebrating life's gifts and preaching God's acceptance – for the rest of his life. Whatever his disciples may have misunderstood or misconstrued about him, they understood and remembered perfectly this teaching: Grow up and live generously toward others, as life has been generous toward you. Do not allow oppression to harden your hearts, narrow your minds, or make you cowards. Do not hold onto life so tightly that you never actually have it or live it.

NOTES

1. Marcus Borg, *Conversations with Scripture: The Gospel of Mark* (New York: Morehouse Publishing, 2009), 40.

2. Loretta Dornisch, *A Woman Reads the Gospel of Luke* (Collegeville, MN: Liturgical Press, 1996), 171.

3. Amy-Jill Levine, *Short Stories by Jesus: The Enigmatic Parables of a Controversial Rabbi* (New York: Harper Collins, 2014), 87.

CHAPTER 15

Jesus in Jerusalem

For many years, preachers have been haunted by two questions: How do we preach the affirmations of the Christian scriptures to the very people who are skeptical about religion? And how do we understand that despite their skepticism, people still want to hear the story of what Jesus' followers believed really happened when he entered Jerusalem on the last week of his life?

I n his book *In the Beauty of the Lilies*, John Updike spoke about what happens when people lose confidence in their religious beliefs but do not lose their desire to believe. He understood this dilemma better than most modern writers. Updike's story begins with a Lutheran minister who – by the turn of the nineteenth century – has read all of the Biblical scholarship available to him at that time. He concludes that there is nothing to the story of Jesus, or for that matter, nothing to the story of God. Though his congregation professes to believe, he decides that religion plays little more than a ceremonial role in their lives.

Rather than settle for a career of preaching what he suspects neither he nor his congregation really believes, he decides to leave the ministry and pour his energies into encouraging the quest for practical knowledge. He devotes his life to selling encyclopedias. He wants to substitute the acquisition of new information for the traditional comfort of a religious faith. But he finds that his quest for knowledge still does not answer his most aching questions.

Even in his atheism, he wonders, "What part of me is sacred and separate from that which gets defined by other people? What is there to live for? What can make me happy?" Knowledge has not brought him the answers to these questions, and he has discarded religion. Furthermore, he discovers that most people are not even interested in knowledge but only in their own personal security. Out of his ambivalence, he leaves a legacy of confusion and depression for his children.

His children devote themselves to the pursuit of security if not success. They do tolerably well, but there is still something missing for them, something that once enabled their father to stand up and sing, "Alleluia, Hosanna. Life is good, God is good. Easter Sunday's promise has been fulfilled." They cannot manage that affirmation, and their focus on personal security only leaves them with the fear that one day they could be left feeling insecure. Their generation has left for itself and its children the legacy of believing that life is what it is. Take it or leave it.

The third generation found the idea that "life is what it is" too boring a reason for living. They became entranced with the idea of celebrity. This generation became hypnotized with the idea of becoming "somebody." Perhaps really becoming known, becoming talked about, and becoming envied was where salvation lay. The former Lutheran minister's granddaughter in particular fought and slept through all of the steps it took to become a successful movie star with multiple apartments on both coasts and reporters constantly inquiring about her life and career. But she left her son with the impression that becoming "somebody" can also be a hollow, almost dehumanizing quest.

That son, now the fourth generation, was raised by a mother whose life's ambition was to conquer the world of fame and celebrity. Her capacity for affection was deeply divided, if not often absent entirely. Her son sought desperately for something more real, more tangible, more loving than his parents' rather casual, preoccupied affection. Gradually, then more strongly, he found himself drawn to a fundamentalist Christian cult. In the latter part of the twentieth century, he had brought the faith circle to a close by embracing the faith that his great-grandfather had been unable to sustain in the face of science and encyclopedias.

Updike's point is that the story of what happened between Palm Sunday and Easter has power far greater than any questions about its historical accuracy. It has power because it asks us to answer the questions: What is important to live for? What in the end gives us a genuine impulse to believe that there is good news to be found in human life, greater news even than the thought that we may yet live another day and that spring will come again, greater news even than the possibility that security, success, or even celebrity will come into our lives? People keep coming back to this Jerusalem story despite the fact that it is built on one of the most intriguing mysteries of history. How can a story have such a profound significance for the Western world when we cannot find empirical proof that much of it actually happened?

The gospel accounts of Jesus' last week are powerful and very easily preached. But even though they carry the power of stories that have passed through the fire of many tellings, they are not history as we understand it. None of the gospels was written by an eyewitness to what is described. Only Mark's gospel seems close in origin to the generation that witnessed Jesus' life. Mark – as well as the other gospels – was written by people who were so desperately involved in the early struggles of Christianity that it was impossible for them to have an objective point of view – if, in truth, they really wanted one.

From fairly reliable sources, we know that Jesus entered Jerusalem, that he was beloved by a group of disciples, that he was executed, and that his disciples believed that his body disappeared. They thought he went to be with God in heaven. The gospel accounts that we have so far were also written by people who lived through the split that took place among Jesus' followers after his death. The split aligned those who understood themselves to be the Jewish followers of the Rabbi Jesus and those gentile followers who, over time, came to resent the Jews for not embracing the new, non-Jewish faith that they believed Jesus intended.

The winners of that struggle, who were gentiles and later to be called Christians, wrote the gospels. They cast blame for Jesus' death upon the losers, who were Jews.

Furthermore, all of the gospels were written after the Romans had become the undisputed tyrannical rulers of the Jewish land, having ruthlessly destroyed any opposition. Any suggestion in Christian writings that the Romans had executed Jesus because they were uneasy about what he was teaching or because they thought he represented a threat to them would have placed the Christians in a very dangerous political position in the Roman Empire. Thus, the Jews were blamed for killing Jesus – igniting centuries of anti-Semitism, the consequences of which we know all too well. Those elements of the story that suggest Jesus came to rebuke the Jews and was killed by a resentful Jewish mob are pro-Roman propaganda and almost certainly not true.

Preachers don't like to interfere with a storyline that they know people want to hear at Easter time, and telling the truth could land them selling encyclopedias – or life insurance – as it did the character in Updike's book. But the traditional story has been responsible for endless misunderstanding, prejudice, and even considerable bloodshed.

Jesus was Jewish. I recently spoke with a priest who told me that whenever he teaches this one fact alone, there are people in any given class who will never forgive him. But it's true. Jesus was Jewish. Most of the Jews in his time neither supported nor condemned him. They did not have the power or the inclination to put him to death, much less crucify him. Crucifixion was a distinctly Roman punishment. All of the gospels are written as if these facts were not true, but they are true.

What's most important is that this story has power despite its counterfeit elements. Jesus did go to Jerusalem. What drew him there? What was he trying to accomplish? What message was he trying to sail in the midst of overwhelming power and oppression? Why was his message remembered? I will do my best to provide a possible answer.

Shortly after Mark begins his story of Passover week, he tells us that the first thing Jesus did in Jerusalem was to go to the Temple. It was not only a place of worship; it was also a national monument that had taken eighty years to build and at various times may have employed over 1,800 men. It was the center of politics and commerce as well as of religion for this part of the world. It was a sign of everything in which the privileged world believed.

From the Roman perspective and that of their hand-picked Jewish officials, the Temple was also the anchor of a pecking order that was fundamental to the Roman economy. Land was heavily taxed to support the empire. People who had wealth, paid taxes, or had political connections had status. Everyone else bore the burden of Roman taxation — which means that the peasants lost their livelihood when the taxes became so great that landowners stopped employing them. Peasants were considered people of such inferior status that it was almost an unclean act to associate with them.

When Jesus appeared to be attacking the Temple, he was challenging a political system that held people in despair and told them they had no right to anything like happiness. Those in the lower orders were made to understand that they were alive at the whim of the Roman Empire that believed peasants were entitled only to whatever best they could make out of misery.

The Romans had seen many dangerous peasants rise up and try to lead a rebellion. They had thought John the Baptist was one, and Jesus claimed some allegiance to John. What they didn't realize was that Jesus had no intention of leading a political revolt. As he stayed in the Temple and answered questions during that Passover week, it became clear that the Kingdom of God he had in mind was a kingdom of personal integrity rather than a kingdom of political dominance. He said repeatedly, in so many words, "Some say the kingdom is here. Some say it is there. Some say it is coming. I say it is here now. It is within you." (Luke 17:21)

Jesus believed that God was no respecter of status. God was not interested in the old purity laws that left some people forever unclean in the eyes of the righteous. God did not have a set of hoops that had to be jumped through in order for anyone to be redeemed in God's sight. God did not behave like the Romans or like anyone associated with the Romans. God was a radical accepter and lover of human beings. Jesus' disciples found this easier to believe, but they experienced this radical acceptance through him.

When the lawyers showed Jesus a coin with Caesar's image on it, they were trying to trap him into denying the value of taxation, which would have been a politically volatile gesture. Instead, Jesus answered quite directly by suggesting that the coin with Caesar's image belonged to Caesar, and taxation had nothing to do with anything that pertained to God.

The Romans weren't inclined to subtle distinctions. Either you went along with politics as usual without a fuss, or you were a political enemy. They couldn't understand someone who stood apart from the system of status, apart from the system of privilege, apart from the payola of politics or from the politics of cleanliness or uncleanliness, apart from religion as it had always been practiced.

As far as they were concerned, Jesus was just another troublesome Jew. Every Passover week for years past, there had been a few Jewish leaders who had risen up and demanded attention. They were routinely arrested and then executed, which usually put an end to their movement. None of them were ever remembered long.

However, the memory of this Jew would be less easy to eradicate. Yet the Romans would not learn that until later. What Jesus offered, and by force of his personality apparently conveyed, was a sense of God's unconditional acceptance of every human being. This acceptance brought to each person a feeling of self-possession and therefore of calm and a sense of peacefulness that overcame whatever the world brought to bear. All that was required, as Jesus said, was the readiness to appreciate the gifts of God that were already given to each person: the gifts of sun and air, food and companionship, service and discovery, but most importantly the gift of freedom from the standards, distinctions, and chains that were forged by the people in power for everyone else to wear.

Yet, the overriding question remains: Why does Jesus' message – contained in a story that is still largely unverifiable – continue to haunt us?

In Updike's novel, the patriarch of the family who is a Lutheran minister abandons his faith because he finds that it conflicts in some ways with the findings of history and science. His children and grandchildren try to be fulfilled with what can be proven beyond a doubt by all of the standards that their societies knew – security, success, celebrity, and freedom.

None of these pursuits brought them any real peace or sense of satisfaction.

This left them, and all of us really, with a story that would not go away – the story with a conclusion that all of us are held in love by the Creation that gave us birth, that all of us have gifts far transcending the status to which others may have consigned us. It is the story of a man who lived his beliefs with serene confidence – and this much we know is true – even to his death. The fact that we hold on to this conviction, that we are loved and worthy of being loved, leads me to suspect that something in this and many other religious stories is profoundly true.

CHAPTER 16

The Easter Question

When visitors attended the congregation I served with the thought of perhaps eventually joining, they almost always ask, "What do you believe about Easter?" I believe Easter is the celebration of something that really happened. What precisely happened is something we will never know. Those who have essentially an "Easter faith" will celebrate in one way, believing that the disciples' account fills their needs. Others will observe the rebirth of Spring – which may or may not actually be happening at this time of the year – and they will discount the Christian story.

I believe something happened that empowered Jesus' followers, men and women who had little or no experience of courage or leadership in the face of danger, to establish religious communities in his name. We may never know what happened, but the story must be taken seriously. What follows is how I understand it.

Have you ever wondered if God is real or perhaps just a product of our wishful thinking? Hundreds of years ago, Jesus' disciples wondered just that. They were looking for proof that the God to whom they had been faithful would lead them out of their captivity to the Roman Empire. What kind of captivity was it? They were heavily taxed. The burden of paying those taxes made it all but impossible for any but the richest and most well-connected to own anything. As a result of this economic system, the vast majority of Jews were poor and getting poorer.

Their poverty stole their sense of dignity, and it created tensions that tore at the fabric of the Jewish community. While a few wealthy families lived comfortably off the labor of others, the vast majority was crushed economically and politically. They half longed for some proof that God cared about them, and they half nourished a cynicism that, of course, God did not care.

Then they encountered a traveling teacher who reflected an extraordinary amount of self-possession. He seemed to understand them without needing introductions or explanations. This intimate understanding was a quality they ascribed only to God. Their teacher's touch was also healing.

Although in this world there was every good reason to be afraid of what other people thought of you, he moved among them confidently – without fear. How could he do that? How can an individual live without some fear of very real threats to his life and well-being?

This traveling teacher empowered people who had thought there was no good in them to believe that they were beautiful in God's sight. He was even thought to have healed some people of serious diseases. It was not even so much what he said. Later, his disciples would have some difficulty remembering precisely what he had said to them or what he meant by it. Rather, it was his manner of being among them that seemed to give his life and their lives a greater sense of purpose.

Some began to whisper among themselves, "Could it be true? Could this man be the Messiah, the man destined to lead us out of slavery? How else can we understand his complete lack of fear for his own safety and well-being?" They began looking for signs. They asked him to declare himself. He would not. They kept looking for wonders, for miracles, which would become part of the proof they needed. Later, they would think that they had seen miracles. News of those miracles spread far and wide, so that others would appreciate that perhaps the Messiah was at hand and would be near when Jesus needed them.

It is difficult to imagine a more combustible situation than the beginning of Passover week – the observance of the Jews' liberation from slavery – when this man entered Jerusalem while being proclaimed by some of his disciples as the next liberator of the Jews. To make matters worse, he went directly to the temple of Jerusalem, which was owned and operated by powerful people.

At the temple, he challenged those who were making money from the spiritual needs of other people. He spoke of the temple, God's house, as if it were his own, and he called those who were making money off the spiritual needs of others "robbers." This was too much insult for the ruling powers to bear, and they put into motion the events that would end his life.

By the end of the week, the cross had claimed another victim. The crowds that had greeted Jesus' entry had gone away. They had been looking for proof of the miraculous, but it didn't happen. There was no earth-shattering victory over death. So, they went on to other things hoping to forget or at least get over their disappointments.

A handful of women – or maybe just one, the accounts weren't clear – came to the tomb where Jesus had been placed in order to be sure his body would be buried properly. And they discovered that his body was gone. The Gospel accounts make it clear that at first, they assumed Jesus had been taken, possibly by grave robbers, and hidden somewhere else.

There are many different ways of looking at what happened next and what it meant. This is mine: The Gospel accounts eclipse subsequent events into a few days, though it was probably months. The disciples' hopes were dashed. The proof they had been seeking – the signs of God's miraculous power over Rome – had not been there. Now even the body of their dear friend had been taken away and probably defiled. And they themselves were wanted men and women. They left Jerusalem attempting both to hide and to get on with their lives.

Then, somehow, they felt they were being drawn back to Jerusalem. They could not get over the feeling that when they were together, he was still with them. It was difficult to put into words. But to explain to a skeptical following what was in their hearts, they told at least ten very different stories of actually seeing Jesus after his death. Most of these stories had one common quality. The disciples had not recognized Jesus at first. They had spent a good deal of time with him before they knew who he was.

The disciples had been skeptics themselves. They had believed his existence in their lives was over. What they reported is that Jesus approached each disciple according to what that disciple most needed to hear, see, or feel in order to be convinced. In other words, the reappearance of Jesus took place spiritually in their hearts rather than physically as they had expected. And they felt it most importantly when they were together. Now, it was not physical proof they even cared about anymore but the spiritual presence – they believed of God – in their lives.

One story in Luke tells us that on the Sunday after Jesus' death, several women came to the tomb and found his body gone. They asked the two men who were standing there where the body had been taken. One man responded, "Why do you seek the living among the dead?"[1]

This was the disciples' way of saying, "This is not about bodies. We don't know where the body is. We don't care. This is not about ghosts. This experience we have had is about a living presence in each of us."

Luke goes on to tell the story of two disciples who were walking away from Jerusalem and talking about the events of the last week. Along the way, a stranger joined them. They spent a companionable day together, and when evening came they sat down together for a meal. At the moment they broke bread, they recognized that the stranger they were eating with was Jesus.[2]

This story may have been their way of remembering that Jesus' presence did not come to them as individuals. After his death, no disciple ever encounters Jesus alone or even suggests this can be done. It is through their common meals that they realized something uncommonly supportive was working through their lives.

How do we know that these stories are not just a reflection of the disciples' own anguish and despair – their hoping for a reassurance that never really came? The survival of the early Christian community against all odds, wrought as it was by men and women who had not been daring or imaginative before then, is a fact which suggests that something very powerful happened to them.

What emboldened very ordinary men and women to become a community of Jesus' disciples in the midst of a political climate that was harsh and threatening to their very existence? It was not a ghost but their sense of his presence – a presence they had never known before – giving them courage and a sense of hope. They thought it might be God's presence.

So, Easter is not about stones being rolled away from openings of caves. It is not about spectral evidence. It is not about empty coffins or mysterious shrouds. Easter is about the presence of reassurance in the lives of the disciples – and whatever reassurances have come into our own lives. It is about our conviction that our lives have meaning and that we will find a way somehow to serve that meaning even after some of our darkest moments.

Easter is the knowledge that those whom we love never entirely leave us and that we never leave them now or in any life to come. It is the recognition that despair never gets the final word. It is the recognition that what "helps and heals and holds us," the presence we seek, reaches out to us best when we are gathered together.

In some years here in New England, we celebrate Easter when it is warm and sunny and there is promise in the air, on the ground, and in the trees of even more pleasant days to come. It is easy at such times to celebrate the birth of new life, the miracle of spring, the wonder of growth. However, in other years, it becomes clear at Easter that winter has not yet given up its grip on our region – as it seems sometimes not to want to give up its grip on our hearts.

Of course, we yearn for warm days and the earth giving forth all of its beautiful fragrances and colors. But we could celebrate Easter in February if we took the occasion to remember and celebrate those times in our lives and in the lives of those we love when the tomb was opened not to eternal life necessarily but to a life reclaimed, a life renewed, and a life rededicated to better things.

NOTES

1. Luke 24:5

2. Luke 24:13-35

CHAPTER 17

That Love Passage

The early church was a fractious bunch of folks, some of whom believed that Jesus' teachings had liberated them from the usual decencies and humilities of human life. The man we called Paul believed he was tasked by Jesus to form these would-be disciples into groups that best understood and attempted to live out the good news that Jesus taught. Some of Paul's task is covered in the book of Acts and the rest in letters Paul wrote to several congregations that he was tending, mostly from a distance. Among these were the people of Corinth to whom he wrote two published letters.

When couples come to me to plan a wedding, they frequently request what they call "that love passage." Some are not sure if it's from the Bible. Some believe it was probably written by Shakespeare or perhaps Ben Franklin. Others remember it's in the Bible, but they aren't sure which testament it's in or who said it. They do remember these words: "Love bears all things, believes all things, hopes all things and endures all things." This haunting passage from 1 Corinthians 13 has been called "Paul's hymn to love."

We often read it at weddings, but every time I read it, I am aware there are some verses that are now very hard to understand. For instance, the writer affirms, "Even if I give up my body to be burned but have not love, it would gain me nothing." This passage has a meaning, but time has made the meaning unclear to modern ears.

The standards set by phrases such as, "Love is patient, love is kind. It does not envy, it does not boast, it is not proud. It is not rude, it is not self seeking, it is not easily angered, it keeps no record of wrongs," are raising the bar pretty high for most of us. Much of the time, we are not that good. Whenever a couple requests this passage for their service, I find myself wondering if they know what they are doing.

So I used this passage with caution over the years until my colleague Rev. Marjorie Rebmann helped me to see things differently. Here is her story.

Marjorie got a new program for her computer. Through this program, she could speak into a microphone that was mounted on a headset, and her words appeared on the computer screen. There was no typing involved, just dictating. The program is called "Dragon Naturally Speaking." I'm sure you've seen it advertised. Now, Marjorie believed that Dragon would allow her to dictate sermons, memorial services, and weddings into the computer so that she could cut in half the amount of time it ordinarily took her to type everything using a keyboard.

The night she installed it, she learned that in order for the computer to get to know her voice, she would have to read to it for half an hour. She chose to read from a book titled *Dave Barry in Cyberspace,* thinking that Dragon would enjoy hearing more about its own world. Here is the story in Rev. Rebmann's own words:

> Dragon has some Buddhist leanings. To start it, you only have to say, "Wake up!" To stop it, you have to say,

"Go to sleep!" To erase a word, you have to say, "Scratch that." So I sat for an hour (talking into) a headset, characteristically slurring my words, saying, "Scratch that," going back, saying the same words over again, and periodically pouring another cup of tea.

When that was over, the program asked me to further refine its recognition of my voice by reading some passages of my (own) work with words that I normally use. They were fairly easy words, like "peace and freedom, soul and spirit, justice and mercy, compassion and forgiveness, committee meeting and potluck, grace and faith, and, of course, Canvass Sunday."

Dragon inhaled my voice and memorized my speech pattern. I was ready to roll about nine thirty, so I decided to write a wedding that was scheduled for the coming weekend. The bride and groom had requested 1 Corinthians 13. Gingerly, I whispered into the headset, "Wake up." Nothing happened. Waking sleepy dragons is the stuff of fairy tales and myth. I had to say it much louder. "Wake Up!" Then I read.

"If I speak in the tongues of men and of angels but do not have love, I am a noisy gong or a clanging symbol," I said. But apparently Dragon had not quite registered my speech pattern. On the screen before me slowly appeared the words, "If I speak in the gongs of mortal sand angels' butts do not have love, I am a noisy gong or a gang symbol."

"And if I have," I said, "prophetic powers and understand all mysteries and knowledge, and if I have faith so as to remove mountains but do not have love, I am nothing." Dragon wrote "miseries" for "mysteries" and "legend" for "knowledge." But I pressed on. Around ten o'clock the phone rang as I was working, and I hollered for someone to get it. I was interrupted again by someone in the house asking where something was. I continued with a couple more interruptions and no little frustration at the words that were appearing on the screen.

I decided to read it all over since I had fixed the thing about "mortal sand and angels' butts." I read from the screen. "Love is patient. Will someone get that damned phone? Love is kind. Why should I know where your new CD is? Who was your servant last year? Love is not envious, boastful, arrogate, crude." Not only were the words scrambled, but I had forgotten to put Dragon to sleep whenever I spoke to anyone in the house. Every word I said was being recorded.

Dragon went on crooning about love. "It does not insist on its own way. "Play that CD a little lower please. I gotta get this wedding done. "It is not irritable or resentful. It does not rejoice in mongering (meaning wrongdoing) but rejoices in the truce."

That's how a computer chip reminded me about religious living. A tiny opalescent crystal grown in a lab somewhere preached a whole sermon to me in my own words. I've always deeply appreciated the language of 1 Corinthians 13, a brief notebook on how to recognize love and how to practice it. Entwined in its classic lines now were the everyday, practical words of frustration. Reading the passage over was somehow hilariously moving.

Corinthians is not a collection of pixels on a plastic page but one of the sanctuaries of the soul to which we retreat when we want to be assured of how to live best in the world. Only we can give the words their value, and only we can live them into meaning.[1]

In the arcane world of Christian theology, scholars used to teach that 1 Corinthians 13 was really a description of God's selfless love of Christ and through Christ for us. Maggie brings this passage right down to the plane where all of us struggle with the guilt we feel when those we deeply care for also have the capacity to frustrate and irritate us royally.

Despite lofty interpretations of scholars down through the centuries, I am now convinced that this question of sustaining normal human love through the ordinary push and pull of daily life was precisely the dilemma that Paul had in mind when he wrote this Chapter 13 of his letter to his congregation in Corinth.

To make matters complicated, the people in Corinth were not, actually, a great congregation. We ministers would have called that congregation "a minister killer," because every member of the congregation thought he or she should have been THE minister.

Those who thought they could preach thought they could probably preach up a storm better than anyone else in the congregation. Others thought they could teach better, plan better, or lead better. They thought they were wiser, humbler, more charismatic, or more favored by God. They were so constantly in each other's faces that they were all "elbows and knees," pushing and shoving each other out of the way. Arrogance and pride ruled the day in Corinth.

How will Paul address this? First, he speaks to those who fancy themselves preachers. He tells them that no matter how much they may think they are God's gift to oratory, if they do not love or respect the people who listen to them, they are like a "sounding gong or a clanging symbol."

Paul tells those who think they are the world's greatest executives and planners that if they have no love or respect for those for whom they plan, their work is worthless. He tells the conservatives in the group that while their unquestioning faith in the "old ways" is laudatory in its way, if they have no real caring for others, their faith won't do anyone any real good. Finally, he says to those who boast of their humility that even though they may make the ultimate expression of that humility by throwing their bodies on the fire to honor some great cause, it will be a worthless gesture without love.

Then Paul goes on to describe love both in terms of what it is and what it is not. The "is not" part is what sounds extremely demanding to us, but it is important to remember to whom Paul was writing. When Paul tells us what love is not – envious, arrogant, rude, selfish, irritable, self-righteous – he is specifically reminding the people of Corinth that they have been all those things and more, and they know it.

But for the rest of us – when we read this passage – we know we have felt traces of those negative qualities in our own relationships with those we love. Who here can really say they have never been envious, arrogant, rude, selfish, or irritable with someone they have loved? No one can say that.

Paul is not talking about fleeting moments of enviousness, arrogance, rudeness, or anger, which most of us do experience even in our closest relationships. Paul is talking about what usually characterizes our relationships with people. Do we really hope for their success as equally as we hope for our own, or would we sort of prefer that they fail – at least a little – so that we can look better in comparison to that failure? Do we really regard other people with as much reverence and wonder as we do ourselves? Can we extend the same compassion to others that we hope to receive for ourselves?

Love means truly wishing the best for other people. It means hoping they can grow to be stronger than their pain. It means we are willing to stand by other people and give them as much strength and encouragement as we can while they wrestle with their own angels and demons. Love means that while we have our moments of anger, frustration, and impatience, we will try to overcome them most of the time. Love means we will have to tolerate occasionally getting hurt, as this is the price we pay for being close to others. But we do not have to tolerate being abused.

Love does not mean that we become blindly trusting. When you are raising children, you realize that in order to demonstrate trust in your children's honesty, you might wish to believe everything they tell you. But there are times when it is also wiser to check things out. The Greek words that were translated, "Love bears all things, believes all things, hopes all things and endures all things" can also be translated into these words: "There is nothing love cannot face; there is no limit to its faith, its hope, and its endurance."

Our deepest convictions and our passing reactions live side by side — often uncomfortably, as Marjorie Rebmann's computer taught her and reminded us. We care very deeply for the people we love, and yet whatever is on the surface of our thoughts and reactions at any given time may not reflect our deepest commitments. If there is love between individuals, then we have to hope that Paul is right and that our caring for one another is stronger than the ways in which we sometimes fail to express it.

In a more recent translation of that famous "love passage," this phrase stands out: "Love never regards anyone or anything as hopeless."

Sometimes we love people when it is difficult to like them. "Love never regards anyone or anything as hopeless," but it is pretty hard to like people who are behaving in an arrogant, selfish, or angry way. Love means that we do not treat bad behavior as if it were acceptable. We do not ignore what we feel needs to be changed. That's called giving up, and "love never regards anyone or anything as hopeless." We may not like some people in our lives, but it is a far more serious thing to give up on them.

What is the effect of all this love, if indeed it exists? How does it rate against having the power to charm audiences, win elections, lead armies, write brilliantly, invent and market a best-selling product, or rising to the top echelons of command in any organization? All things, Paul tells us, will pass away. For most of us, our greatest achievements will be like puzzling reflections in a mirror when at the end of our lives we try to understand what has been most important.

What have we most valued? For what do we most want to be remembered? What will our friends say about us at our memorial service, and what will our children remember years after we have left them? I can tell you the answer to that. They will probably forget the honors we earned and the positions we held, but they will remember the many ways – subtle, direct, or indirect – in which they loved us and we loved them.

Paul concludes this passage, "In a word, there are three things that last forever: faith, hope, and love; but the greatest of them is love." May those we love remember that we believed in them and that we let them know it. That's what love means.

CHAPTER 18

Expecting Miracles

I've always been interested in miracles — not so much those that would catch headlines, should they be reported — but those that happen to most of us quietly but importantly as we live the lives that are given to us. This sermon avoids posing questions such as how the natural order of things could be disrupted for this to happen and instead asks us to reckon whether they do happen to us — and I think they do — and what may be behind it. There may be several answers to that question, and I will give you mine.

A mountain is not a miracle. At least, we would not call it a miracle today. A mountain is a pile of rock that has been thrust into the air by a series of geological movements that we think we understand. Eventually soil forms. Plants and trees grow from it. So, a mountain is like a large biology project: beautiful, complex, intricate, but understandable. That's what we believe.

But Native Americans and folks in other parts of the world used to endow some of their mountains with qualities of the Sacred. Some mountains — Mount Washington, for instance — were once considered off limits to human beings, because they were thought to be holy places. Rivers, lakes, mountains, the sea, and sacred groves of trees in Britain, Scotland, and Wales were thought to be the miraculous dwelling places of the Great Spirits.

A chance encounter between friends is not a miracle. If two old friends suddenly meet unexpectedly, or if two strangers find each other and a sustaining friendship deepens over the years, we would say that is one of those fortunate, random events that make up many lives. "Random," we say, as in haphazard events. These are accidental events, we tell each other. Nothing governs them but statistical probability. Yet when in such a random meeting one or both persons find a missing piece of her life, something she had been looking for and desperately needing to find – perhaps a reassurance or an insight – then the experience does seem close to miraculous.

A long-term, sustaining relationship is not a miracle. It is not a violation of the laws of nature. Anthropologists can tell us why human beings seem to bond with one another. Psychologists have written libraries full of books telling us how to do it. Anyone who chooses may be well-schooled in the science of relationships. Yet, when a long-term relationship continues to work well for both people – despite the occasional frictions, misunderstandings, dark moods, retreats into privacy, all of the changes in the lives of two people, the inevitable temptations, and the equally inevitable fatigue on both people – then such a bond seems almost miraculous.

A work of music is not a miracle. A talented musician can put notes together in ways that form a tune or a complex of tunes that may even become a symphony. I cannot do it, but some people can. What they do is not something we would normally call miraculous. But the tune or the words that catch, hold, and express some vital non-verbal part of our lives or of our lives together seems almost miraculous because of the power of this gift to help us become better or at least more honest than we often are. When Mozart said some of his music and William

Blake said some of his poems seem to have come from somewhere beyond their conscious creating, they were not claiming their work to be superior to that of other musicians or writers. They were saying they could not locate the source of that skill within themselves. It seemed almost miraculous.

But why talk about miracles now? For many people, the world in which miracles were thought possible began to quiver and shake when Darwin's theories of evolution were gaining favor in intellectual circles. If God did not create the world and everything in it, if instead all living things evolved through a process of trial and error, a series of random fortunate or unfortunate encounters, then many people thought there was no place for the miraculous. Life, including human life, was a biology project and nothing more. By the turn of the twentieth century, faith in the miraculous goodness of life had begun to fade like the Cheshire Cat in Lewis Carroll's story of Alice. The cat was there, then it was only vaguely there, then there was only the hint of a smile, and then nothing at all.

Many people then asked, "What will we do? What is there to hope for if the old religious stories and the assurance they gave are no longer true?" And they decided, "We're going to figure it out for ourselves. We're going to put our shoulders to the wheel. We're going to learn the laws of the universe and make them work for us. We no longer have a miraculous God of miracles, but we have human intelligence. We will make our own miracles in science, technology, medicine, art, law, and world diplomacy. We will wed religion to science and philosophy so that religion will no longer need that old tottering, creaky God of miracles anymore. Religion, science, and philosophy will be the engines of human progress." That's what they said.

Why talk about miracles now? Well, we are beginning to discover that when all things have been properly explained and we have been adequately instructed, there are quite a few areas of our spiritual experience that are left uncovered, unexplained, undiagnosed, and mysterious. While we do understand many things, what remains mysterious is what gives us the hopefulness to live well.

We still can't answer some questions. From whence comes the power of goodness and caring when it passes from person to person? Why does this power have the ability to heal – and upon occasion even physically heal – another person? We understand evil. We have all kinds of ways to explain human cruelty. Nothing really explains why the sacrificial care and concern of one person for others can be transforming.

We do not understand community. We have all kinds of theories about why groups work or don't work. We have filled rooms with texts on group psychology and motivation. We don't understand what lies behind the cohesion of a group that accomplishes something far beyond what they would have dreamed.

We do not understand courage. We can understand cowardice well enough, and we can understand the adrenaline that enables people to run into burning buildings to rescue trapped victims. What we do not understand is the prompting of conscience, that moment when an individual is confronted with a burning bush and a prompting to do something very hard and even dangerous. Perhaps no one else knows this has happened, and no one would fault that individual for remaining on the safe side of things. We do not understand what prompts people to risk physical or psychological safety in order to do what they feel is right.

We do not understand chance encounters that seem just what we needed at that time. We do not understand what is happening to us when we feel as if we have been spoken to but there is no voice to be heard and no other person present to be speaking. We do not understand what speaks to us out of our favorite music, art, or poetry. We do not understand what pulls

FRESH WATER FROM OLD WELLS • 151

us to the mountains, to the sea, to the garden, or to the lakeshore. To be sure, there is a desire for peace and quiet or recreation, but often there seems something ineffable, something elusively more.

Many summers ago, my wife Nancy and I had the good fortune to be at the base camp of Mount Rainier near Seattle on one of the few indisputably sunny days they had that summer. The trails that go up into Rainier rise from that base across beautiful, open meadows. So it was easy to watch what seemed like an endless procession of pilgrims heading into the high country. Some were out for the exercise, but many were there to experience something like what the Northwest Native Americans experienced from that mountain: a sense of the miraculous, an encounter with – what, a presence? No, not so much a presence as a calming, healing mystery.

There are a number of things we don't understand and probably never will. Much of what we don't understand after years of rigorous investigation is what encourages, supports, and sustains us in this life. The real source of Nature's strength, as well as our own, is still shrouded in mystery – a mystery that even the most rigorous science can't yet unfold. And because we have a tendency to dismiss what we do not easily understand, we fail to see the miraculous happening all around us. We have been taught that there are no miracles; yet miracles of chance, miracles of serendipity, miracles of love, and unseen strength are all that keep us going sometimes.

Those who wrote the early scriptures were well aware of the mysteries that sustain all life. The mysteries of life were not something that galled or frustrated them. Not having to resolve or explain seemingly chance events of goodness or strength in their lives, they simply loved the mystery and wrote of it in the most extravagant terms.

When Moses was pleading with Pharaoh, did he actually throw down a stick and turn it into a snake? What did happen was that the leader of a group of slaves confronted the ruler of a mighty nation. That sort of courage was miraculous enough. Why not explain it in miraculous language?

Did the Red Sea part to let the fleeing slaves escape through and then close over their pursuers? Perhaps what actually did happen was that a group of people who had become too comfortable in groveling captivity willingly accepted the risks and burdens of freedom in order to gain a new dignity. That was a miracle. Why not tell the whole story in miraculous language?

Did Jesus feed five thousand people with five loaves of bread and two fish? Every time they hear the story, many have the impression that Jesus waved his hand over the five loaves and two fish and created a veritable Super Stop and Shop of bread and fish. We think there must have been fish flopping around everywhere. But what the text actually says is that there were never more than five loaves of bread and two fish. Jesus broke them and distributed them to the crowd. The text reports, "All ate and were filled." (Luke 9:17)

What we assume from this story is that you have to have a heck of a lot of bread and fish to fill up five thousand people. The actual point of the story may be that the quality of Jesus being present in some way to each of those people, distributing small bits of food to each of them, was enough to make them feel full.

Did Jesus turn water into wine at a wedding? How could he have done that? Or was the experience of being in his presence such that it made the water taste like wine? Looking at the scriptures in the no-nonsense way we often do, we tend to seek scientific certainties. Did the Red Sea part for the fleeing Hebrews or didn't it? Volumes of articles have been written to test the literal truthfulness of this story, demonstrating that properly translated it wasn't the Red Sea but the Reed Sea. In other words, it was a swamp that stood in the way. But is that really the point?

The authors of scripture attempted to describe a world they saw as surrounded by a loving mystery. This mystery encourages people to risk everything for freedom. This mystery empowers some people to embody or nearly embody the best that's possible in human nature, a mystery that knits people together, sometimes despite their own selfish or fearful designs.

Probably the skeptical attitude that most of us have developed is necessary in some ways, but it is not the only possible lens through which we can understand our lives nor is it, by any stretch of the imagination, the best lens we have for understanding what makes life worth it. When we view life with a little more poetic imagination, we can begin to expect that sometimes miracles will happen and then be happy when they do.

I know that many have prayed for a miracle cure, and it did not happen. I am not talking about big miracles like a spontaneous cure of a dread disease. I'm talking about the little mysteries of connection between people, inspiration from unexpected sources, courage in those from whom we least expect it, new and unexpected possibilities that open for us just when we have quit looking. I am talking about a sense of acceptance from somewhere that comes to us when we have lost all conscious self-confidence. If we don't expect that these little miracles can happen, then we will never notice when they do happen. Living entirely in the skeptical mode is like turning off your internet and then wondering why you are not receiving email.

Recently, an article in the *Boston Globe* related that Stephen Hawking's ashes have been interred in Westminster Abbey between those of Sir Isaac Newton and Charles Darwin. The internment was followed by a service of thanksgiving for

Hawking's life that was attended by over one thousand people. Apparently, someone had asked the dean at Westminster Abbey who decides such things why one of the world's most famous atheists – as Hawking was – was buried in the Church of England's home parish. The Reverend John R. Hall responded, "Whether a person believes in God or not, if someone is achieving extraordinary things, then I believe God is in that process."[1] I believe that, too.

NOTES

1. Stephen Castle, "Stephen Hawking Enters 'Britain's Valhalla,' Where Space is Tight," *New York Times*, June 15, 2018, http://www.nytimes.com/2018/06/15/ . . . uk-stephen-hawking-westminster-abbey.html.

CHAPTER 19

Your Next Minister: Some Things You Need to Know

After I left parish ministry in Wellesley Hills, Massachusetts, I entered the transitional ministry, which means that I served many congregations who were trying to figure out what they wanted in their next minister and of themselves. Understandably, this was the most requested sermon I ever gave as an interim minister. I should point out that the ministerial settlement procedures may have changed since I preached this, but the issues and questions have not changed.

Many years ago on a Saturday afternoon, I was walking through the Wellesley Hills Unitarian parish hall on my way home. We were hosting a youth conference, and so kids were scattered around the room in small conversation groups. Suddenly one young man, a member of my congregation, appeared at my side to ask me a question. As was his style, it was posed in a semi-humorous way. Although I did not learn it until later, it contained a serious purpose. I was tired. I wanted to get home, and so I kind of tossed his question aside with what I thought was an equivalently humorous response. I thought no more of it.

Twenty-five years later, when I began serving a different Unitarian church, I met that young man again, now married and a father. I wondered why he looked like a thundercloud every time we were near each other. Then one Sunday, he asked for an appointment. We made one. He came into my office and told me he had borne a grudge against me for thirty years. It had been eating at him until he heard something in a sermon I had given that previous Sunday that convinced him I could understand why he had been upset. His question back then had been serious, but I had not taken it so. I apologized, and I was deeply sorry for the hurt he had received. We're friends now. But that incident remains an object lesson.

Every parish minister today is a walking projection screen. Focused upon us are the hopes, wishes, and dreams of many members of the congregations we serve: their visions of an ideal preacher, pastor, or prophet; their hopes for a mother, father, lover, friend, and confidant. We, of course, often cannot know what is projected onto us until we find it out, usually too late.

Along these lines, nearly every congregation that is looking for a minister this year is looking for a community builder, someone who will help them build here in their church the loving, forgiving, indulging, creative, redemptive community that has eluded humankind for generations. This too is projected onto the new minister, and so he/she goes forward carrying the weight of very high expectations.

Today we hope much from our ministers. But until recently, most people expected little of those who climbed into these high pulpits every Sunday. In the nineteenth century, if a family had several sons, they sent the most ambitious sons into the family business. The son who got stepped on by every other member of the family was encouraged to train for the ministry. Consequently, if that young man did one thing in ministry very well, his parishioners were delighted. They expected their parson to be an unworldly sort of fellow. They suspected that was why he had chosen the profession of minister.

For example, William Ellery Channing gave great sermons, but you had to strain to hear them, for he was not a strong-voiced preacher. Those who tried to get to know him often found that the closer they got to him, the more uncomfortable he became. Channing, who spoke so feelingly about love and fellowship, was actually uncomfortable outside of a small circle of his closest friends.

Ralph Waldo Emerson's minister, Barzillai Frost, was a beloved and dedicated pastor, but he had no gift for preaching. His dreadful sermons caused Emerson to comment that while listening to one sermon his mind wandered, and he gazed out the window at newly falling snow. The snowstorm, he recalled, was real. The preacher was not. Despite earning Emerson's obvious contempt, Barzillai Frost was greatly revered by his parishioners as a pastor because he took care of them. In those days, if you could do only one thing well, you were a success in the ministry.

Today, our expectations for both congregations and ministers are so much higher than they ever have been. We come to church seeking a caring community, because our world is so rushed and pulled apart by competing pressures that a dreadful impersonality creeps into the places where we live and work.

We come to church hoping to find support for our individual journeys. Unlike generations before us, we are still convinced that our inner lives should be better. We come to church now looking for the prophetic voice that takes on oppressions that were not even recognized as oppressions until very recently.

We want so much more out of life than generations before us ever dreamed of wanting. We build ourselves up with great hopes and with great potential for disappointment. There are some things you should know and talk about in order to avoid that disappointment so that you can have a satisfying and fruitful relationship with your next minister.

When a congregation in the liberal tradition goes in search of a new minister, its search committee creates a profile of the person they seek. That profile goes onto, for instance, a Unitarian Universalist Association or a United Church of Christ website where any minister can read it. To register an interest, a minister just clicks on the congregational profile, and his/her name will be sent there. I call this time "the fishing season," because the line of every congregation goes into the water at the same time, and everyone waits for nibbles. And the UU fish are biting in November.

Periodically, I go to one of the websites and read the profiles from some other congregations who also have their lines in the water. The profiles I read are amazingly consistent in what they want.

They want everything. They want a great preacher. They want a person of solid intellect, considerable passion, and commensurate speaking ability. But this person must be comfortable speaking to and satisfying a congregation of theists, Christians, humanists, pagans, Hindus, Buddhists, Jews, Sikhs, Druids, as well as those who have no use for religion but attend for the coffee.

They want a dedicated and caring pastor who has solid administrative skills. They want a spiritual guide who will also understand fundraising and help them increase their annual budget. They want a team builder who will be able to resolve staff conflicts by getting every staff member to agree and get along most of the time.

They want a harmonizer, a builder of community who is still able to lead in those new directions that will "grow" the church, but not at the expense of anyone who wants the minister's attention. They want a social activist who can represent the congregation to the community, but only on those issues around which everyone in the congregation already agrees. They want someone who absolutely adores little children, teenagers, and retired folks. In fact, one congregation put it almost exactly that way.

Of the profiles I read, all of the congregations want and believe they should have all of those qualities in their next minister. Several warn that should they call a minister claiming to have such a package of qualities and then discover that they were wrong, the disillusionment will be great and terrible to behold.

Now this is the point where we all nod sagely and reflect that we would never expect a minister to be all things to all people and that we have to expect that our minister can get only so many things done in a week. We do believe that, but do we really feel that way? When the minister upsets us or people we care about, do we – at that moment -- really remind ourselves that we were not looking for someone who would please everyone?

My first point is that you will never find a minister who can fit even fifty percent of that profile. God or Nature – take your pick – does not distribute equal helpings of those prime ministerial qualities to any one individual. The minister who moves smoothly through crowds and loves being constantly with people will probably not be the preacher who will bring fresh provocative ideas to a congregation. They're two different personalities. They have different, almost opposite gifts, and those gifts do not reside together as strengths in most individuals.

The dedicated pastor everyone wants will very likely not pay the same attention to staff issues or team building that she pays to visits and hospital calls. The social activist may be drawn away from working with young children or reaching out to teenagers by his commitments to leading change in the community. The collaborative facilitator that so impresses the congregation at first may turn out to be not quite the leader it needs. And the energetic leader to whom everyone was initially drawn may be more of a powerhouse than the congregation bargained to get.

Every congregation wants and believes they deserve to have something they imagine is "the complete ministerial package." Some parishioners tell me, "Well, we had that complete package once in Reverend X, and we just want another Reverend X." Frequently, I knew Reverend X and strongly suspect that his or her memory has become idealized even in a short passage of time since his/her departure.

The idea of a complete package is an illusion. Everything we know about the development of personality reflects that having some qualities as strengths precludes having other qualities as strengths. Good ministers learn to maximize what they do well, compensate for what they do not do as well, and the congregation learns to fill in those areas where the minister alone cannot meet every conceivable need. That's why good ministers are successful. They have the help of the congregation to compensate for what they do not do well.

So, the complete ministerial package is an illusion. It doesn't exist in anyone. What a congregation needs to do is determine where it most needs strengths in a minister. Then it needs to find that minister or ministers who have those strengths, call one of them, and then figure out how the members can fill in the rest.

Let me briefly summarize. You will not get all of the requisite ministerial qualities in one person, and that does not mean you have a defective minister. It does mean that there is plenty of room for the ministry of the congregation to take hold and do very exciting work. You will not get someone who will be a perfect fit. You will not get someone you will fall in love with right away, nor will you find someone who will be able to love you right away. It takes time.

Now, I have two questions for you to think about. How much of a leader do you want? Do you want a minister who is significantly out in front of the congregation with new ideas and new directions? Do you want to be challenged in that way? Or do you want someone who works behind the scenes building consensus until there is clearly no significant opposition to a new direction. Let me remind you that leaders have a tendency to want to change things, and I haven't yet noticed that change is high on most lists of favorite values.

I have to tell you that the research on congregations of average size suggests that you do need a minister who is visionary, who has hopes and dreams, and has a direction in which she or he is prepared to lead. That sounds fine in principle, but it does create friction. Do you want your minister a little bit ahead of the pack, creating friction but possibly in the interests of building a more vital role for your congregation? Or do you want your next minister building only upon the foundation of what nearly everyone now believes? I cannot answer that question for you, but it will be a major issue for your next minister.

My second question is: Do you really want your next minister to have definable beliefs? Do you want your next minister to have beliefs with edges, with limits, beliefs that mean one thing and not everything? Many congregations do not. There are some ministers who come close to preaching sermons that employ a potpourri of vague beliefs, but I think they leave some people wishing their minister had offered more clarity as to what their particular version of "good news" really is.

What happens when a minister lays out a specific definable belief? Some people will agree; some people will disagree. Can you stand to disagree with your minister without losing faith in him or her? Can you make the tension that real diversity creates work for you?

I think some of us hope to find some friction against which we can begin to clarify our own ideas and commitments. And I think ministers are supposed to offer that friction sometimes. So I hope you will welcome those areas in which your next minister clearly stands out from the crowd, because he or she has a point of view that is independent even from most people in the congregation. Welcome those discussions as an opportunity to get to know your minister better and as a chance to get to know yourself better by entering into the dialogue.

Finally, I meet twice a year every year with eighteen UU ministers who formed a study group thirty-eight years ago. They are, by any criteria, experienced and successful ministers. Some of you who know them respect them, as I do. As I looked around our circle, I realized that half of the ministers there had been fired once in their careers. They were not fired because they were incompetent at ministry. In each instance they were fired because ten to fifteen members of a congregation they served dedicated themselves to forcing the current minister out. Each minister believes he or she could have won a congregational vote, but ten to fifteen determined people can make a ministry unsustainable for everyone.

I realize that little failures and some big ones are built into every modern ministry: the sermon that didn't gel on Saturday night or on Sunday morning either; the snap judgment that opened up an unexpected can of worms; words said in pastoral counseling that were misunderstood and felt to be deeply wounding; thoughts spoken in a moment of fatigue or distraction that alienated a powerful supporter; a hospital visit to a critically ill parishioner that was missed because it came at the end of a busy week.

In addition, there is the inevitable failure to be what individuals really want you to be: the projection of someone's mother, father, former pastor, or former lover; the projection of someone's idea of a perfect healer, pastor, preacher, prophet, or community builder; the projection of someone's idea of the perfect minister.

We ask our ministers to embody the highest ideals we can imagine. While we claim we know that nobody is perfect, and we understand that everyone makes mistakes, we really don't want our ministers to walk over our illusions and projections by making those mistakes. Therefore, failure is inevitable. I'm aware that failures happen in everyone's life, but I believe our hopes for modern professional ministry are so far off the charts that ministers will fail them routinely.

Since ministers have also bought into those impossibly high hopes at some level, they will be just as disappointed in themselves as their parishioners sometimes are in them. Thus, the modern professional ministry is made possible only by strong lay members who are able to be critical when necessary while remaining supportive of their minister as a person with strengths and weaknesses.

Whatever names are on the list that you will get this year, I know that Peter Pan's name will not be there. There is no magical ministerial pixie dust that can take you to "Never-Never Land" or make this the institution it wants to be without a great deal of hard work on everyone's part. It will be all of you, working together in ministry, along with your very flawed and wonderful new religious leader.

CHAPTER 20

Mr. Dickens' Holiday

A Christmas Carol by Charles Dickens is considered a classic not only of his literature but of all Christmas literature. He wrote it at a time when his future as a successful author was in question. Since the season for bringing out Christmas stories is short, he wrote quickly in hopes of achieving a modest success. The words seemed to flow onto the paper; this is because significant parts of the story are autobiographical. Dickens knew his characters more intimately than many readers supposed.

I n 1843, Charles Dickens published a short novel that could have ruined him and sent his family into poverty. He paid for the full cost of publication. Even his publishers no longer had any confidence in the manuscript because he was writing a Christmas story about death, ghosts, haunting, poverty, and despair. It was called *A Christmas Carol.*[1]

To begin, there was not a large market for Christmas stories. Christmas was not a major holiday in the 1840s, and it was not a holiday at all for the poor. Rich people used it as an excuse for a sort of high-class orgy. But when Ebenezer Scrooge reluctantly gives his clerk Bob Cratchit the day off to celebrate Christmas, and Scrooge grumbles Cratchit is robbing him of that day's pay, he is not alone in that attitude. Many middle- and working-class people in England felt or had been treated the same way. Scrooge also spoke for many people when he called Christmas a "humbug."

The Industrial Revolution was in full swing. Profits were in the saddle. Many people worshipped progress and the accumulation of wealth. The poor had to scramble to get whatever security they could find, or they would be forced to accept the meager comforts of imprisonment in poorhouses for their debts. For all classes, religion had become like a beloved but irrelevant great aunt. It's nice to have "Auntie" around, but of course, we all know she is hopelessly old-fashioned and out of date.

This was the culture for which Dickens wrote *A Christmas Carol*. Ebenezer Scrooge seems a caricature to us, but Dickens' readers knew him very well; many even recognized him in themselves. And they knew the Cratchits. They had seen hundreds of Tiny Tims live briefly and then perish for lack of adequate care. The story was an arrow aimed straight at the conscience of Victorian England. For a young man who desperately needed to sell a successful book in order to feed his family, it was a brave but very risky public statement that there is a higher law than profits.

To remind you, the story begins on Christmas Eve. Scrooge is falling off to sleep after a long day at the counting house when suddenly a dreadful apparition appears to him. It is the ghost of his dead business partner, Jacob Marley.

Marley is wrapped in chains that hold locked strongboxes. He has been condemned to roam the earth that way, seeking in death the chances he passed by in life — the chances to lighten the load of his fellow men and women. Marley has come back to give Ebenezer one last chance to avoid the same fate. Scrooge will be visited that night by three ghosts: the ghosts of

Christmas past, present, and future. Marley urges Scrooge to go with them and see what they have to show him.

The Ghost of Christmas Past takes Scrooge on a tour of his own growing up. He sees himself again as a lonely boy whose closest companions were his books. He remembers longing for the presence and warmth of real people in his life. He encounters himself as a youth, sent away from home by his father. But now, his sister has come to get him on Christmas Eve. He remembers his hopes for the love and approval of others – hopes buried long ago because they were never realized.

As he watches the scenes of his life pass by, Scrooge sees the many people who actually did reach out to him – people who desperately tried to slow his long slide into self-absorption. He remembers a young woman with whom he had been very much in love but whose soul he could not reach because he was so preoccupied with his own financial security. She told him, "You fear the world too much." Scrooge is quite shaken by these scenes as they bring him memories of the opportunities he missed because of risks he would not take.

Soon after the first ghost leaves, the Ghost of Christmas Present arrives and takes Scrooge on a tour of his acquaintances' homes. It is Christmas morning. He visits the home of his clerk, Bob Cratchit. There, he experiences the warmth and stoic bravery of this large family as they make the best out of what they are able to afford on the wretched salary Scrooge pays. He hears their expressions of kindness toward him, a kindness he doesn't deserve. He sees, as well, their worry over the fate of Tiny Tim, their sick youngest child.

Scrooge then visits the home of his nephew, and he realizes that this young man embodies all of the love that Scrooge once received from his sister before she died. On both of these visits, Scrooge is made to realize that even as hardhearted as he is now, some people have not given up on him.

The Ghost of Christmas Future is the most frightening specter of all. It has no face. It does not speak. It merely points. Scrooge sees the Cratchit family wearing down in their struggle against poverty, living now without Tim who has died for the lack of medical attention they could not afford.

Scrooge also visits the bedchamber of a man who apparently died in his sleep. The maid and the cleaning lady are dividing up his things before the undertaker arrives. Two business associates down below in the street are arguing over whether it would be seemly to have a funeral at all for this man, since no one would attend. Scrooge asks, "But who is this man?" He is taken to an untended grave in an out-of-the-way cemetery. The specter points to the headstone that bears the name "Ebenezer Scrooge."

As morning dawns, Scrooge realizes that he has been given a reprieve. He has been given another chance to live his fullest humanity. What has changed Ebenezer Scrooge? It's fair to say that three ghostly visitors in one night would change almost anyone. But we are led to believe that it was what Scrooge saw in those visits that changed him. He saw love struggling to survive within his own life. He saw a chance for that love to be rekindled. He saw the elemental efforts of other people to keep their basic humanity alive within a dehumanizing culture. He saw that the bottom line for everyone is that nobody lives forever. The journey of life is brief, harder for some than for others, and hardest on those who try to make it alone. He saw that the only antidote to a freezing death of the heart is a generosity of spirit toward other people.

This story saved Charles Dickens' faltering career. Although he wrote many other Christmas stories, he never could create the effect of this one. Why did it succeed against all odds? I think there are two reasons. The first is that the author knew the darkest regions of the human heart intimately, and he knew that the struggle against the death of warmth in the soul is the hardest battle we ever fight. He knew it because he had been there. In real life, Charles Dickens was Ebenezer Scrooge. The story is autobiographical. Dickens was a young man when he wrote it, but he could sense that Scrooge was growing within him and would, in later years, threaten him with Scrooge's emotional isolation.

Dickens had a hard life as a child. Like Bob Cratchit, his father was a clerk. But Cratchit was the father Dickens never had. His own father was irresponsible with both money and love. The family lived hand to mouth, moving every other year or so. John Dickens was imprisoned twice for debt during his son's childhood. During one of those imprisonments, twelve-year-old Charles was taken out of school and put to work in a factory. He lived in a small room that was near where he worked. Both parents freely spent money they didn't have. Neither seems to have understood or loved their eldest child very much. Dickens once wrote:

> I was not beaten or starved; but the wrong that was done to me had no intervals of relenting and was done in a systematic, passionless manner. Day after day, week after week, month after month, I was coldly neglected. I wonder, sometimes when I think of it, what they would have done if I had been taken with an illness; whether I should have lain down in my lonely room and languished through it in my usual solitary way or whether anybody would have helped me out.[2]

The young Scrooge, alone in his room with books his only company, was the young Charles Dickens in reality. His only playmate and the joy of his life was his younger sister Fanny. The character in the story named Fanny comes to fetch Ebenezer Scrooge home on Christmas Eve. In the story, Fanny is the mother of the nephew who tries to cheer him up. Fanny in the story is the dear sister whose death Scrooge never got over.

Fanny, in real life Dickens' own sister, died five years after the *A Christmas Carol* was written, leaving a crippled son.

Unlike Scrooge, Dickens was neither friendless, single, nor childless. But like Scrooge, he carried with him such an overriding concern for his own personal security in the world, such an overwhelming need for power over others that he was incapable of emotional intimacy with his wife, or, it would seem, with most of his children.

Unlike Scrooge, Dickens was an extraordinarily generous man with his time and money. He supported friends and family heavily, contributed to charities, and campaigned for laws to benefit the poor. He never forgot where he came from or how hard his life had been. Like Scrooge, however, his grudge against the world and his inability to forgive those closest to him had become an obsession which kept from him what he most wanted: the security of being at the center of a genuinely loving family.

A Christmas Carol was successful for two reasons. First, its power comes from the fact that it is the young Charles Dickens seeking a salvation in fiction he never wholly got out of life. The second reason is that many of us recognize the struggles of Ebenezer Scrooge from our own experience. Dickens is offering us a chance to look into his mirror and see ourselves.

Have we been bruised in our growing up? Have we held on to that anger and focused it sometimes on the people who are closest to us? Have we ever turned aside offers of friendship or kindness out of an unreasonable fear of entanglement with other people? Have we ever accused the world of doing to us what we are actually doing to ourselves?

Scrooge lives in a prison of his own devising. The doors are shut and sealed with a fear of the world he will not let go. His chains are forged with regrets he cannot release and hurts he cannot forgive. What the ghosts had done was give Scrooge permission to release the locks and chains and go back to the world that needs the care and love of all of us.

Dickens' story shaped the celebration of Christmas both in Great Britain and America. The British and particularly Americans latched onto this story because it transformed Christmas from a dull ecclesiastical holy day to a celebration of the possibilities of human warmth and hope. And there is something else you should know about Dickens' contribution to Christmas.

At about the age of thirty, Dickens himself decided he could not accept the indifference toward the gospel of love, compassion, and service to others that he had learned from his parents' Anglican faith. So he joined a Unitarian chapel. In the interests of full disclosure, at the conclusion of his life he was nominally an Anglican again. But his most beloved work, *A Christmas Carol,* was written just after he became a Unitarian, and it reflects his new liberal religious commitment. This is our story.

Early in the story, Jacob Marley tells Scrooge, "It is required of every (one) that the spirit within should walk abroad among his fellow men and women and travel far and wide." This is a fundamental liberal religious idea. Life is a great gift that comes to each of us from many sources. Every one of us bears a portion of that gift, and it is our responsibility to walk among our fellow men and women, giving whatever portion of strength, encouragement, advocacy, or support we have in ourselves to give.

Later in the same section, Scrooge tries to comfort Marley who seems to feel his life has not been well lived. Scrooge says, "But you were always a good man of business, Jacob."

Marley replies, "Business! Humankind was my business. The common welfare was my business; charity, mercy, forbearance and benevolence were all my businesses. The dealings of my trade were but a drop of water in the comprehensive ocean of my business."

All of us in liberal religion believe that the business of humankind — the real sum and end of living — is that we try to do as much as we can to make life easier for those who travel with us. The journey of life is brief. It is harder for some than it is for others, and it is hardest for those who try to make it alone. We have this major responsibility to give each other warmth and company.

Finally, what moves us about this story is that Dickens, like many other liberal religionists of his time and ours, believes there is always another chance for us to lead lives more in line with our best ideals and hopes. In the great economy of life, no one's best efforts are lost unless we somehow conspire to lose ourselves. Even then, there is always a way back. The heart of this story — the heart of the Western Christmas too — is the belief that no matter what darkness lies within us, we can overcome it.

NOTES

1. All quotes from *A Christmas Carol* in this chapter are from the following edition: Charles Dickens, *A Christmas Carol* (New York: Barnes and Noble, 1994).

2. Charles Dickens, *David Copperfield* (Peterborough, Ontario: Broadview Press, 2001). Dickens often inserted autobiographical reflections into his novels, particularly this novel. Nearly all contemporary biographers believe this passage is Dickens speaking about himself.

CHAPTER 21

Reflections on a Journey

I once served a congregation in transition that was following a program of monthly themes around which the worship services and programming might be arranged. Since I wanted to conform to this practice as much as reasonable, I wrote the following reflections on "Life's Journey," the theme of the month.

It was just the second day that we were newly minted hospital chaplains. We were looking forward to another comfortable day of orientation and donuts. But instead, our supervisor said to each of us, "Here are your four assigned wards. Go out there and be chaplains."

We were stunned. That was it? No further training? No more pep talks? No tips on how to talk to patients or doctors? No more donuts? Just go up there and do it? But it was time. Much of ministry is on-the-job training with time for reflection later, and we were now officially on the job.

Somehow, I pushed myself into the room of my first patient, who was an elderly man. I introduced myself and asked if I could be helpful to him. He said calmly, "Well, sir, I am 86 years old and full of cancer." Just like that. He waited to see what I might have to say, and of course, I had nothing to say.

It was the first time I had ever met anyone who consciously faced his own imminent death, and I had no idea what to say. I think I tried to reassure him that I would have the chaplain come up and see him, and then I turned to leave. Shutting the door gently behind me, I suddenly realized, "Wait a minute. I am his chaplain!"

By the time I returned to that ward, my first patient had gone home. I was relieved when I learned this, because at that stage of my preparation, I was not able to help him. By the end of my internship, however, I knew a few more things. I had studied with Dr. Elisabeth Kubler Ross who was doing groundbreaking work on the needs of dying people. I now knew about denial, anger, bargaining, and depression – some of the phases of grieving a serious loss.

I was ready to get down in the trenches with the recently stricken, but I had not been ready to help the first patient I had interviewed. He and I were at different stages of our own journeys. He had apparently made peace with a life in which his own days would soon come to an end through a wasting disease. And I – who was really just starting out – was not yet ready to talk with someone who had accepted that the end of his journey was now so near.

I do believe that each life is a journey during which we learn some things that carry us through our days. We also learn and discard other ideas and skills that don't have the same lasting strength. We learn that horizons we were once afraid to cross are eventually immanently crossable to someone with a little curiosity and a lot of courage. Each horizon crossed leaves us changed; we will never be quite the same again. We will probably be stronger and wiser but also more careful and a little more cautious about who and in what we believe.

At the start of our lives, we learn to walk, talk, and ask for what we want. Gradually, we learn that we must give up the idea that we can have anything we want just by making a fuss about it. As we discover that not everything is possible, we also discover that there are boundaries that delineate what is right and wrong for each of us. Perhaps every child needs to learn two things couched one way or another. The first is that you really are special to your parents. The second is, "But get over yourself. You're not that special!"

When we're young, we can become very adamant about what we think is right or wrong for us. But over time we realize that other people have their own boundaries, and we must be as firm in respecting their boundaries as we are about our own. Gradually, very gradually, what adults call "the sacredness of other people" begins to dawn on us. And when it does dawn on us that all people carry something of the sacred, then we cross yet another horizon that slowly changes our outlook on life.

When we reach the point at which we want to compete on sports teams or gain the attention of other people who don't need to like us for any reason, most of us discover – though I'll admit that some never learn this – that there are times when to achieve what we want, we have to meet the expectations that others have of us. In so doing, we find out that what others want of us is not so unreasonable. We discover that our lives are filled with other people who really may even have something to teach us.

Somewhere, we discover that every journey – including our own personal journey – has an end. We call it death. Knowing that death awaits us, we also know we do not have forever to achieve what we hope and dream. At some point in our childhood or young adulthood, we may have thought we were immortal. Eventually, we understand that is not so. In that understanding, life becomes infinitely more precious. At some point, we learn that other people are as complex and vulnerable as we are. It is funny that we hadn't figured that out earlier, but perhaps it took a little more appreciation of the value of each person's journey to make the point clear to us.

What many of us also learn as we get older is that preoccupation only with ourselves is a very dusty, lonely road to be walking for the rest of our lives. I certainly remember when as a young man I was besotted with a certain writer of immense novels detailing the glory of the objectivist spirit, a celebration of self-interest according to the doctrines of Ayn Rand.

As time went on, I learned that life does not work itself out that way. Sooner or later, we need each other for warmth, support, and understanding. This requires that we learn to be sensitive to the hopes and needs of others. We learn this because we now know there will be an end to our journey, and we may want some company in approaching that end.

On this life's journey, we discover that it is a wonderful achievement to do something well, to have some accomplishments of which we can be proud. Then a few years later, we discover there are people who can do some things better than we can, and it is usually better to let them go to work. There are younger people who have the energy we used to have – though maybe not yet the same wisdom – and it is wisest to give them our blessing going forward. For what we are learning on this journey is that we create many of the barriers that haunt us. As our time grows shorter, we learn how much love is there for all of us in the end, even despite our fears and shortcomings.

Finally, we know that throughout the journey we take, there are an incredible number of good things that have happened to us without our having to do too much to make them happen. There are people who stood by us through good times and bad. Their love and loyalty were particularly strong when we felt least worthy of it. There were also beautiful days and beautiful moments that pulled on us even when we were beset by the problems that darken everyone's life by seeming sometimes to be bigger than they actually are.

At the end of our long journey, we want to be able to say –
as we have heard others say – that we've been incredibly
blessed beyond anything we ever thought we deserved. We will
all come to that final reckoning – if not with God, perhaps then
certainly with ourselves.

In recognizing the many losses that are a part of each
journey, I realized a long time ago that surviving each loss and
incorporating some lessons and perhaps some toughness into
our lives are important parts of everyone's growth. It's possible
that feeling homesick was one of our first losses. Life continues
to bring the inevitable number of setbacks that we must face
and deal with.

As my career in ministry progressed, I became fascinated
with all of this. Eventually I wrote a small book of lectures
questioning whether our religious movement took losses
seriously enough. It was published, and many Unitarian
Universalists read it.

Suddenly, I was becoming a loss consultant for our
denomination and getting calls from all over the country. I was
getting tired of loss. I wanted to stop thinking about losses and
start thinking about gains. I decided to do a sermon about what
happens when people receive sudden wonderful gains along
the path of their journey. I found a study done on former
lottery winners.

We used to believe that coming into a lot of money too
quickly can ruin a person's life. That old suspicion can be true if
the people who receive the money are haunted by the feeling
that they really do not deserve it. If they think they do not
deserve the money they won, then they cannot spend it out of
their lives fast enough. As long as they have the money, it
rebukes them. It speaks to them of their unworthiness. On the
other hand, those who won the money but understood that
their new fortune only meant that they got lucky and that they

didn't have to deserve anything to be lucky, they were more able to live comfortably with sudden good fortune.

Then I realized that this same dynamic applies to journeys that are afflicted with sudden losses. Those who understand that bad things just happen to some of us without our having deserved them have a much easier time getting over their losses. But if we think there is some reason for that loss – something we should have done differently – then we will waste important time reexamining the past, looking for evidence of the mistakes we think we made that caused us to "deserve" what happened.

I don't know why, but we seem to feel responsible for all the bad things that happen on our journeys. We will even invent mistakes we did not actually make in order to prove there was a connection between our loss and something that shows we deserved it. On the other hand, believing we were just unlucky can alleviate the amount of time that we carry our pain, though it doesn't make any loss less painful at the time.

If you were brought up in certain religious traditions, this is hard to accept. You were brought up believe that God created a system of rewards and punishments that explain everything that happens. Looked at in this way, a catastrophic earthquake, flood, or illness is God's way of expressing displeasure.

A colleague once told me of a time when a Lutheran minister asked if he, my UU colleague, would officiate at a funeral service for a member of his Lutheran congregation. My friend agreed. In the tradition of UU ministers, he set about trying to find some good things to say about the deceased. He found out that the man was sort of grumpy and generally disliked, but he had a very intriguing inner life, had written poetry, and kept an inspiring diary. My friend gave the eulogy using these sources. He thought he had done a wonderful job. But at the end of the service, the congregation filed past him with nary a smile or even a "nice service, Reverend," which usually means, "I slept through the whole thing."

When all was over, he went to the funeral director and asked, "What went wrong?" The funeral director said, "You crazy Universalist. Don't you realize that they all hated the man? They came to the service only to hear the minister declare that he was at that moment boiling in the fires of Hell."

That won't happen here. Rest assured that when you reach the end of your journey, we will only say good things about you.

In the book of Job, God tests a good and honest man. The things that happen to Job could only happen in our worst nightmares. So, Job questions God about his bad luck. What did he do to deserve this? God reminds Job that for all of the bad things that happened to him that he feels he did not deserve, there were many good things that happened to him, and he didn't deserve them either. Often there is no reasonable explanation for how our journeys progress, for what we lose and what we get. But the beauty that comes our way for free and without our deserving it is a large part of life's meaning and happiness, even sometimes in the midst of pain.

At this stage of my journey, I will cast my lot with the teaching that what life has already given most of us may be a whole lot more valuable than what we deserve. Yes, we have lost and will lose good friends. But did we really deserve to have them? Were their contributions to our lives pure gifts — gifts that were given to us without any question of our deserving or not deserving those gifts?

Think about it. Would you really want a world of pure justice in which every quality would be doled out to us in proportion to our own behavior? Drivers who never yield the right of way would never get to make a left-hand turn. People who are constantly critical of others would find that others were constantly critical of them; they would never hear a kind word.

Those who are taciturn or shy would encounter people who were equally uncommunicative; they would never actually have a conversation. Those who always need to be the center of attention would never find anyone else interested in paying attention to them.

Would you really want a world with that kind of justice? Would we really want the world only as kind to us as we are kind to others, only as tolerant of us we are tolerant of others? While we will feel there are folks who fall below our standards, we know full well there are other people whose graciousness to us far exceeds anything we ever thought we deserved or meted out to others.

There is no question of our deserving what happens when a great and unexpected sadness hits us. Probably we didn't deserve it. But the great moments we received of happiness and peace that come upon us — we didn't really deserve them either.

These thoughts might not come to us at all if we were not fully aware that our journeys would come to an end — an end at least to life as we know it. In the knowledge of that end, we look at life's gifts with an entirely different level of appreciation.

Of course, we do not know for sure what is beyond that last horizon. Here are some things we generally must take on faith. Death is either an extinguishing of consciousness without pain, hurt, or terror, or it is just finally peace. Perhaps the final phase of our earthly journey is only the beginning of a longer journey, another form of consciousness that we cannot yet begin to understand. Many people in the congregations I served have had hints that such a prolonged journey may be real. Members of my own family have had experiences that lead them to believe that death is not an end. It is my faith that our journey does not end; it does not have to be your faith.

The following poem is attributed to Henry Van Dyke and many others. It is possibly the most requested reading I have shared as a UU minister:

I am standing upon the seashore. A ship, at my side, spreads her white sails to the moving breeze and starts for the blue ocean. She is an object of beauty and strength. I stand and watch her until, at length, she hangs like a speck of white cloud just where the sea and sky come to mingle with each other.

Then someone at my side says, "There, she is gone."

Gone where?

Gone from my sight. That is all. She is just as large in mast, hull and spar as she was when she left my side. And, she is just as able to bear her load of living freight to her destined port.

Her diminished size is in me – not in her.

And, just at that moment when someone says, "There she is gone," there are other eyes watching her coming, and other voices ready to take up the glad shout, "Here she comes!"

And that is dying ...[1]

And that is living.

NOTES

1. The poem "Gone From My Sight" was probably written by Rev. Luther F. Beecher, who lived 1813-1903. However, it is widely attributed to Henry Van Dyke by Barbara Karnes who included the poem in a small blue book she published in 1986. Poem text source: https://allpoetry.com/Gone-From-My-Sight.html.

ABOUT THE AUTHOR

Known as an inspiring preacher, Dr. John Hay Nichols is now Minister Emeritus of the Unitarian Universalist Society of Wellesley Hills, Massachusetts, where he served as senior minister for twenty-three years. He also served as interim minister for ten other congregations in Massachusetts, Rhode Island, and New York.

Rev. Nichols holds a Doctor of Ministry degree from Meadville Theological School in Chicago and has taught at Andover Newton Theological School and New York Theological Seminary. He is also the author of *A Wind Swept Over the Waters, A Biblical Humanist Companion, Liberal Religion's Response to Loss*, and *Lives that Speak and Deeds that Beckon*.

Made in the USA
Columbia, SC
01 November 2019

82393759R00108